The Good, the True, and the Beautiful

For
Dave and Hailey Jackson
Teresa Luna
Ken Childs
For helping us to think on these things
1 Corinthians 1:3–5

The Good, the True, and the Beautiful

MEDITATIONS

Harry Lee Poe
Rebecca Whitten Poe
EDITORS

CHALICE
PRESS
ST. LOUIS, MISSOURI

Cover and interior design: Elizabeth Wright

Visit Chalice Press on the World Wide Web at
www.chalicepress.com

10 9 8 7 6 5 4 3 2 1   08 09 10 11 12

Library of Congress Cataloging-in-Publication Data
The good, the true, and the beautiful: meditations / edited by Harry Lee Poe
and Rebecca Whitten Poe.
    p. cm.
Includes bibliographical references and index.
ISBN-13: 978-0-8272-1252-7 (alk. paper)
1. Meditations. I. Poe, Harry Lee, 1950- II. Poe, Rebecca Whitten. III. Title.

BV4801.M45 2006
242—dc22

                                                    2006028828

Printed in United States of America

Contents

Contributors

DAVID COOK is a fellow of Green College, Oxford, and holds a dual appointment as Holmes Professor of Faith and Learning in the philosophy department of Wheaton College. Cook is the founding director of the Whitefield Institute, which researches in theology, ethics, and education. He is the author of *The Moral Maze*.

DAVID DOCKERY serves as president of Union University. He serves on many boards and is the current chair of the board of the Council for Christian Colleges and Universities. He is the author of many books, including *Biblical Interpretation Then and Now; Christian Scripture: An Evangelical Perspective on Inspiration, Authority, and Interpretation;* and *Ephesians: One Body in Christ.*

DONALD DREW has been involved in InterVarsity Christian Fellowship for many years in the United Kingdom. Educated at Cambridge University, Drew worked for many years with Francis Schaeffer at L'Abri. A former lecturer in English at the University of Kent, Drew is author of *Images of Man: A Critique of the Contemporary Cinema.*

NIGEL GOODWIN is the founder and director of Genesis Arts Trust, a London-based ministry committed to serving the needs of Christian artists, actors, and performers throughout the world. A graduate of the Royal Academy of Dramatic Art, Goodwin also founded the London Arts Centre Group. After studying theology, Goodwin spent several years in the L'Abri community with Francis Schaeffer and Hans Rookmaaker.

JAMES JONES serves as Anglican Bishop of Liverpool. He has special interest in urban regeneration, the role of the voluntary sector in community renewal, the value of the family to social cohesion, and the engagement of Christian faith with contemporary culture. He chairs the Governing Body of St. Francis of Assisi City Academy and is the author of several books, including *People of the Blessing, Jesus and the Earth,* and *Why Do People Suffer?*

RICHARD LLOYD-MORGAN serves as Chaplain of King's College, Cambridge. A baritone opera soloist of long standing, Morgan formerly served as priest at St. Paul's, Clapham, within the greater London area.

FREDERICA MATHEWES-GREEN is a popular speaker and author. She has served as a regular columnist and commentator for *Christianity Today* and National Public Radio. She has written several books, including *Real Choices: Listening to Women, Looking for Alternatives to Abortion,* and *The Illuminated Heart: The Ancient Christian Path of Transformation.*

BEN PATTERSON serves as campus pastor at Westmont College and has served on three occasions as conference pastor of the C. S. Lewis Summer Institute. A contributing editor to *Christianity Today* and *Leadership,* he has written *Serving God: The Grand Essentials of Work & Worship* and *Waiting: Finding Hope When God Seems Silent.*

JOSEPH PEARCE serves as writer-in-residence and professor of literature at Ave Maria University in Naples, Florida. He also edits *Saint Austin Review,* a trans-Atlantic monthly cultural review. His biographies of leading Christian figures include *G. K. Chesterton: Wisdom and Innocence, Tolkien: Man and Myth,* and *Solzhenitsyn: A Soul in Exile.*

HARRY LEE POE holds the Charles Colson Chair of Faith and Culture at Union University in Jackson, Tennessee. He also serves as program director for the triennial C. S. Lewis Summer Institute in Oxford and Cambridge. Poe has served as a pastor, prison chaplain, denominational executive, and academic administrator in the past and previously taught at Bethel Theological Seminary (Minnesota) and The Southern

Baptist Theological Seminary (Kentucky). He is the author of many books and articles including *See No Evil, The Gospel and Its Meaning,* and *Christianity in the Academy.*

REBECCA WHITTEN POE is a senior at Union University in Jackson, Tennessee. Salutatorian of her graduating class from Madison Academic High School in Jackson, Tennessee, she won the silver medal in literature in the national Academic Decathlon competition in 2005. She studied at Regent's Park College of Oxford University during her junior year. Rebecca is coeditor of *C. S. Lewis Remembered: Collected Reflections of Students, Friends, and Colleagues.*

VISHAL MANGALWADI is an international lecturer, social reformer, and political columnist for the *International Indian.* Mangalwadi is the author of ten books, including *The World of Gurus* and *India: The Grand Experiment.* His current project is related to the Bible as *The Book that Shaped a Millennium.*

RICK WARREN is the pastor of Saddleback Church in California and the author of *The Purpose Driven Life, The Purpose-Driven Church,* and many other books. Warren's ministry has influenced thousands of churches and millions of people.

Acknowledgments

This collection of meditations comes from the sixth triennial C. S. Lewis Summer Institute conducted in Oxford and Cambridge from July 24 through August 5, 2005. Many people contributed to the times of worship from which these meditations come. We are most grateful to the Reverend Brian Mountford, rector of the University Church of St. Mary the Virgin in Oxford, for his hospitality in welcoming us to his church for our opening and closing services in Oxford. Our morning meditations in Oxford were held each day at St. Aldate's Church, and we are grateful to the rector, the Reverend Charles Cleverly, and to Anya Herklots for allowing us to use the church and for making our stay so inviting. We conducted our opening service of the Cambridge week at Ely Cathedral, where Canon David Pritchard and Janet Leebetter arranged for us to take part in Sunday Evensong. Our morning meditations in Cambridge were held each day at the Faculty of Music Recital Hall where George Brown and Alex Kidgell provided for us. The closing service of the conference was conducted at King's College Chapel through the courtesy of the Reverend Richard Lloyd Morgan, Ian Thompson, and Sarah Fowell.

Morning worship times were led each day by the Reverend Dr. Ben Patterson, the conference chaplain. The Institute Chorale Director was Dr. John Dickson who was assisted by Dr. John Hollins and Mrs. Amber Fort-Salladin. Kim Gilnett served as liturgist for our worship services.

The summer institute required three years of planning and the involvement of many volunteers and staff of the C. S. Lewis Foundation. The Program Planning Committee included Stan Mattson, Gayne Anacker, Jill Fort, Nigel Goodwin, and Todd Pickett. Sharon Helton served as director of conference services.

Donna McDaniel served as events manager. Larry Linenschmidt served as house manager. Katie Ward, Melanie Jeschke, and Lesley Anne Dyer served as information and hospitality coordinators prior to and following each service. Jonathan Wright served as technical director for the services, and Jean Rowles served as stage manager. Videographers included Art Batson, Ralph Linhardt, and Stephen Halker.

We are most grateful to Dr. David S. Dockery, president of Union University, for his support of our involvement in the work of the C. S. Lewis Summer Institute. Mrs. Marjorie Richard offered extremely helpful assistance in the preparation of this manuscript. Dr. Trent Butler of Chalice Press recognized that these meditations could serve a wider audience. We appreciate his efforts on behalf of this collection and his patience in waiting for the final draft. Finally, we are grateful to the John Templeton Foundation for their grant in support of the 2005 C. S. Lewis Summer Institute.

Harry Lee Poe
Rebecca Whitten Poe
Union University
Jackson, Tennessee

Foreword

The conference theme "Making All Things New," led me to think about the great apostle Paul living in the Roman city of Philippi. For preaching the gospel in that city, and having the courage and the common sense to be politically incorrect, Paul was summarily incarcerated in one of Emperor Nero's prisons. While there, far from being silenced, let alone being crushed, he triumphed over physical and mental suffering for the name of Christ. Not from a home, but from a prison cell, he cheered and rallied his fellow believers, while his circumstances were in striking contrast with the freedom of his Christian experience. In the future—I have particularly in mind younger people—it will be the same for us. Christ has made us free, but political crises may bring personal danger and even loss of physical freedom.

In our time, should one not relish the privilege of being able prayerfully to study a letter like this and to identify with Paul's willingness to endure ignominy, shame, and pain—and simultaneously be grateful to God? When in the right relationship with God through Christ, we are empowered to make a lasting contribution to those things that are truly worthy of reverence, respect, and honor—those things that ring true. It's hard to find them in these days, sometimes; but there are things that ring true that make for right, for wholeness, for wholesomeness—things that are pure, lovely, lovable; actions and activities that are kind, generous, winsome, that are pleasant to hear about and prompt us to give thanks and to commend.

Now these days, how essential is a living, daily commitment to these God-given truths when, for example, we consider the prevalence and availability of abortion or pornography, in addition to the daily torrent of filth on TV that can overwhelm our lives and take them over? We endure a ceaseless flow of distraction and subtly corroding, sensual excitement. With that disposable, ephemeral and often even babble from Bedlam endeavoring to overtake and overwhelm our lives, it is far from easy to hear, let alone listen to, that still small voice that graciously persists in speaking about truth, meaning, and purpose. We need to have a subconscious awareness of our weaknesses and susceptibilities and of Satan's devices, and to be truly sensitive to the Holy Spirit's presence within us and to God's promptings, continually taking firm, decisive actions to protect ourselves, our families, and our friends.

Paul rightly insists that if there is any value in virtue, in excellence, in anything worthy of commendation and praise, then we should at once think about, weigh up, deliberately activate our wills, pray about, emulate, and see that our conduct conforms to those things. In other words, wherever virtue is to be found, let those things be the basis of our thinking and of our behavior. Words alone are quite insufficient and inadequate to commend the gospel. It is the living that tells—or it does not tell. But it has to be observed moment by moment, something that is consistently attractive each day. The daily living of the gospel should not only commend it to unbelievers and almost-believers; such daily living should provide some of the indelible hallmarks of what constitutes authentic, Christlike living and testimony, in the ups and downs and unexpected messes of daily living. Such attributes should and must daily shape our thinking and be transferred, translated, into attitudes and actions.

Does not God command it? Did Paul live it? He did. So can, and must, each one of us get up and go on.

Paul is writing to believers who are enduring steady privation and outright persecution, just as many folk in the worldwide Christian family, day in and day out, courageously continue to endure. This is not yet every believer's daily and nightly experience, but throughout the whole of the running centuries, God's people have not only anticipated the possibility of persecution, but have expected it as a fact of Christian life. Day after day they were to prepare their minds and wills for it. Is that surprising? It should not be, even though sometimes it is hard to realize it. C. S. Lewis phrased it well, "Christians live in enemy-occupied territory." We should expect daily attacks and, eventually, especially for the younger people here, persecution. What Paul is saying positively is this: Do not let yourselves be shaped by the prevailing culture. Through thick and thin, hold on to those things that are true and lovely. Let them shape your attitudes to people and things, whatever the circumstances are.

And so in daily life, whatever is happening, we believers should be exhibiting integrity of character and a gracious nobility of life, prizing each fragment of human worth and claiming that for God, while in the process asking the Lord to go on making all things new—and new in us: our character gifts, our creative gifts, our spiritual gifts.

The God of the Bible goes on revealing in love, and wants to reach out to us believers in all our broken humanness to make us fully human. It is not optional. It is required that we show folk outside Christ what being fully human is. What a privilege! What an honor. Let us never apologize or trivialize the gospel. It contains all the truth any man or woman, boy or girl, needs to know. As the shadows of evil, unbelief, confusion, despair, and scorn magnify, then let us be sure that as pilgrims we continue, along with the next generation and the little ones following behind, with bold encouragement to keep the flag of truth flying, until the day comes when each of us lays it at the Lord's feet.

Donald J. Drew

University Church of St. Mary[1]

As Noah shut the doors to the ark
while the city went about its business,
the usher shut out the noise and traffic,
the peering eyes and curious gazes
of casual pedestrians and tourists,
while the fumes of gasoline and diesel exhaust
rose toward heaven in place of prayers.

University Church of St. Mary
Oxford
July 24, 2005

---

[1]Poems preceding chapters are all by Harry Lee Poe.

Introduction

Harry Lee Poe

The sixth triennial C. S. Lewis Summer Institute took as its theme "Making All Things New: The Good, the True, and the Beautiful in the 21st Century." We chose the theme to address a major issue facing our culture. The kind of social and cultural chaos that C. S. Lewis predicted in *The Abolition of Man* came in right on schedule in the closing decades of the twentieth century. Relativism reigned supreme. The idea of any sort of objective values or absolute point of reference seemed "absolutely" medieval to the popular mainstream culture embodied in late night television.

We knew what we had lost and what we might still lose in a society that refused to acknowledge "the Tao" about which Lewis wrote. It seemed odd, perhaps, for Lewis to choose a term from Chinese thought to express what the Western philosophical tradition refers to as "natural law," but Lewis chose his words wisely. He wanted a word that embodied the notion that the sense of moral absolutes has a universal dimension that creates a huge historical, anthropological, psychological, sociological, and biological problem for the champion of naturalistic explanations for all of human experience. Lewis did not use a Christian

1

term. He used a term from a distant culture that grew up independently of the Western tradition.

Lewis gave the warning in *The Abolition of Man,* but he gave the warning so that we would do something about it. The C. S. Lewis Summer Institute gathers "mere Christians" together every three years for two weeks in Oxford and Cambridge to stir one another up to creativity to make a constructive contribution to our culture from a Christian perspective. For our 2005 institute, we gathered to consider how Christ might provide a way out of our relativistic quagmire. The postmodern mind has largely rejected the ways of modernity. The postmodern critique has had a devastating affect on the rationalistic, deterministic, materialistic tradition of the modern world. For the most part, however, the postmodern critique took place without reference to Christ, since the modern world banished Christ first of all. Whether the French Revolution, the Russian Revolution, the Freudian revolution, or the Darwinian revolution, the great modern social experiments had no place for Jesus Christ. Postmodernity did not reject Jesus Christ. In a sense, it rejected every "ism" that had rejected Christ. Postmodernism offers no philosophy, belief system, methodology, or value system. Instead, it clears the modern deck and cries out for something else.

Long before the prophets of postmodernity cried out in their Parisian wilderness, Christian thinkers such as Lewis, G. K. Chesterton, and their forebears had pointed out that the modernist emperor had no clothes. Modernity was never a friend to the gospel. It took the devastation of the Babylonian conquest to make Israel pliable enough to be useful once again to God. Babylon disappeared a few years afterward. Perhaps postmodern ideas with their devastating affect on culture will serve the same purpose in the hands of God. After all, it is God who judges cultures and brings them crashing down.

So the six hundred or so participants in the C. S. Lewis Summer Institute gathered to consider the place of values represented by "the good, the true, and the beautiful," in the twenty-first century. Rather than merely mourning what culture has lost, we came together to consider how we might provide light to guide the culture out of its darkness. We came together with the thought that only once in five hundred years do we have the opportunity to play a part in forging a new age like the Medieval, the Renaissance, and the Modern. Postmodernity is not the new age. It was merely the funeral announcement for the failed secular experiment called modernity.

One of the most hopeful signs of the postmodern cry for help is the acknowledgment by the postmodern generation that there is more to life than meets the eye. They are a "religious" generation after the order of the Athenians of the book of Acts whom Paul perceived to be very "superstitious." That is to say, they have a profound sense that life has a spiritual dimension beyond the physical, but like the first-century culture of the Greco-Roman civilization, they do not know what lies behind the veil. The old modernistic apologetic that attempted to prove the existence of God is completely irrelevant for the postmodern generation because they know some kind of God exists. They just do not know this "Unknown God."

While the summer institute heard two plenary speakers every day for two weeks and spent several hours three afternoons a week in focused seminars exploring different dimensions of the problem of values from the perspective of many different disciplines, we began each day in worship. While we strove to address the questions about values that the postmodern generation had raised, we knew that the resources for answering the new questions rested in Christ and the faith we proclaim. We read the scriptures, recited the creeds, sang the songs, prayed our prayers, and heard the thoughts of those who stood before us each morning to guide our meditations. Our speakers represented a variety of traditions within the church—from Orthodox to Catholic to Protestant. Bishops, pastors, theologians, and laypeople took their turn in leading us. This collection contains the words they shared.

The collection begins with a foreword by Donald Drew, now in his eighties, and it concludes with an epilogue by Rebecca

Poe, who was eighteen when she wrote it. Drew represents the generation to whom Lewis spoke when he first delivered *The Abolition of Man* in 1943, and Poe represents the generation with which Lewis was ultimately concerned. Drew grounds this collection in the crowd of witnesses who have gone before, and Poe points us toward those who need the point of reference that Christ provides. Through them and those others who have contributed to this collection, we find a positive word for a desperate generation. The word is not always what we might expect. Sometimes we are surprised. Richard Lloyd-Morgan reminds us that Christ bids us extend hospitality to people who annoy us or whose lifestyles offend us. James Jones reminds us that care for the earth was the first responsibility that God gave us. These and other reminders do not always fit into our attempts to link politics and religion, but these reminders help us recall that the gospel is larger than our political agendas.

Perhaps a final word needs to be mentioned about the poetry. Before each chapter appears a poem. One of the most triumphant acts of barbarism effected by modernity was its success at eliminating poetry from the public square. The odd bird still writes poetry, but for the most part poetry died with World War I. Lewis lamented its death. A popular art form that the mass public enjoyed as entertainment until World War I, poetry has become largely a private matter between the cultural elites. My own little act of subversion is to drop bits of poetry here and there in hopes that it might take seed. People who have lost their poetry cannot read or understand the Bible as God spoke it. God is a poet. The modern world only valued scientific facts. Poetry speaks on a different plane of what science can only imagine.

Between Yesterday and Tomorrow

"Tomorrow is another day."
Was Scarlett O'Hara a pessimist?
What a dreadful thought,
after all that happened today!
More of the same? or worse?

"Yesterday all my troubles seemed so far away."
Blond idiot!
Things wouldn't be so bad today
if you'd only paid attention.

"Today, while the blossoms still cling to the vine,"
is all you have.
Make the most of it.

Jackson, Tenn.
September 26, 2004

Making All Things New

David Cook

TEXT: Philippians 4:8

I wonder what you and your friends and family back home are making of Oxford, the United Kingdom, and the world scene:

Bombings in London. Nothing new there! As it was in the 1940s for Lewis, so it is for us today.

War. War in the world, whether in Germany, France, Russia, Japan, Asia, Europe, or Africa. As it was in the 1940s for Lewis so it is today in 2005 in Iraq, Egypt, Sudan, the Middle East. It is much the same for us today.

Moral change and decay. The collapse of marriage and marriages, a rise in cohabitation, increasing permissiveness. As it was in the 1940s for Lewis, so today in the media, on the Web, and in society more generally it is the same for us.

There is battle between good and evil.

For C. S. Lewis, the background to his work and writing was the struggle between good and evil. For Lewis, the content of his work and writing was the struggle between good and evil. This struggle between good and evil is not just the case in his novels and his science fiction. This struggle between good and evil is not just in his Narnia tales. The struggle between good and evil is also in his academic writing and in his apologetic writing and broadcasting.

It has always been so. In the Old Testament, the people of God and the standards of God were opposed and resisted by the Canaanites, the Babylonians, and the Assyrians. It was a struggle of cultures, a struggle of moralities, a struggle between good and evil all expressed in a world filled with war, a world filled with a lack of security and safety, a world filled with sexual challenges and changes. It was a struggle between good and evil. In the New Testament, the struggle was between the church and the world of the Pharisee, the Zealot, the Romans, and the heathen. It was a world filled with violence and struggle. It was a world filled with decline—both from the glory that was Greece to the later fall of the Roman Empire. It was a world filled with moral decline. It was a struggle between good and evil.

So today there is a struggle between Christianity and the philosophies of the day. Christianity is in a struggle against hedonism, utilitarianism, and subjectivism. Christianity is in a struggle against the social structures of today—the stress on self rather than on community, on rights rather than responsibilities, on demands rather than on duties. Christianity is in a struggle against the moral evils of today with license and a focus on evil as the norm.

We have a choice. Our society has a choice. It is important to express that choice in its starkest terms. It is a choice between good and evil. Shall we say, "Finally, brothers and sisters, let your minds be filled with everything that is false, everything that is shameful, everything that is immoral and tainted, every-thing we detest and disapprove of, with whatever is bad and blameworthy"? Or shall we say with Paul, "Finally, brothers and sisters, let your minds be filled with everything that is true, everything that is honorable, everything that is upright and pure, everything that we love and admire, with whatever is good and praiseworthy" (Phil. 4:8)? "Finally" is a summing up of our duties. It sums up the difference between the right and the wrong kind of life. It indicates a choice of how we should fill our minds. It means be filled, consider, take account of, calculate, count the cost before you commit. It implies that we are not to be ignorant or half-hearted. The emphasis is on letting our *minds* be filled.

Minds matter. Our minds matter because God has one. God is a rational, reflective God. God has given humanity minds. They are given so that we can think God's thoughts after Him. Minds are given to us so that we can be like Him. Moreover, Christ has a mind, and we are urged and entreated to know the mind of Christ. It can be known, and we can know it. We are taught to love the Lord our God with all our hearts and soul and *mind* and strength (Mt. 22:37). We are urged to have the same mind in us that was in Christ Jesus (Phil. 2:5). How can we resist the pressure from the world to conform to its standards? How can we resist being squeezed into the world's mold? How are we to be transformed? It is by the renewing of our *minds* (Rom. 12:2). Notice how that renewal is a communal call for our minds together to be renewed rather than simply an individualistic experience and requirement. We are summoned: "Let your minds be filled." But this is not just talking about our intellect, reason, or brain. We are not just talking about thinking.

The existentialist approach is to state that "to do is to be." The pragmatist philosophy suggests that "to be is to do." The Sinatra philosophy is "Do be, do be, do…"

What we think affects all we do. What fills our minds fills our lives. What we think is expressed in our actions and behavior. Indeed this is how people know what we are actually thinking. What we do reveals our thoughts. We are whole people. Our minds, our attention, our focus, and the content of our concentration—all are expressed in all that we say, do, and are.

So then on what are we to concentrate? With what are we to fill our minds and lives in this struggle between good and evil? We are to concentrate on everything that matters and all the qualities that count in life. How then are we to live? What are we to do, be, say, and think? How are we to behave? The choice is ours.

Everything That Is True

Do we believe what politicians tell us? Do we believe what we read in the newspapers and magazines? Do we believe what we hear on radio and see on television? Is it true? Or is it just my way or someone else's way of seeing and interpreting the world? Is it just the commentator's subjective view, or do we and can we attach ourselves to the Truth? God is Truth, and in science we think God's true thoughts after Him. In art, literature, the social sciences, and philosophy we must be attached to what is true in thought, word, and deed. We must be attached to Jesus—the Way, the Truth, and the Life. Or do we settle instead for what is false and nothing but subjective and error? Fill your minds with whatsoever is true.

Everything That Is Honorable

Paul urges us to fill our minds with whatsoever is honorable. This means with what is venerable, worthy, worth being honored, worth being venerated. It is striking to see that already so soon after the death of Pope John Paul II that the Catholic Church and the new Pope are moving to venerate him as a saint. They consider him worth being venerated. The honorable focuses on what is nobly serious, what exhibits dignity, and what is worthwhile. It does *not* regard what is either shameful or what lacks intellectual seriousness.

Plato and Socrates struggled against the Sophists who simply played with words. The Sophists tried to make the false true and the true false. So much of our conversation tends to focus on the trivial rather than what is honorable. Let your minds be filled.

Everything That Is Upright

Paul adds that we should let our minds be filled with what is upright. Right, being righteous, and living righteously are not very fashionable these days in Christian circles. To live in a right relationship with God means that we must live in right relationships with humanity, the world, knowledge, art, literature, and science.

The word from Paul is steeped in the idea of justice. In our daily relationships we are to live properly, to live justly—to live and do justice. We are not to live immorally, treating people as things or simply as means to our own ends. Other people are not to be vehicles for our own selfishness or for our own pleasure. We are never to treat the world and the animal kingdom as if it is ours to do with whatever we like, instead of a world given to us as stewards and trustees. We are to live in justice and righteousness.

Everything That Is Pure

Paul goes on to say that we should let our minds be filled with—focus, concentrate on—what is pure. Here purity is used in a moral sense. But this covers not just the sins of the flesh. It means that we are to be pure in the whole of life. We are to be chaste. We are to be self-controlled. Paul is stressing that we should "be sinless." To sum up all that he means, we can express the point as, "Be holy." Lewis knew how uncomfortable that makes us.

Many of us have been greatly influenced by J. C. Ryle's book *Holiness.* I wanted to write a book that tried to capture some of what Ryle taught and emphasized. So I thought of titles such as *Back to Holiness, Holiness 2,* or *Yet more Holiness.* The publisher told me that such titles would not sell. Christians today are not really interested in holiness, far less in buying books about it. So I caved in, and the book was called *Wholeness.* This was much more acceptable. To be holy means to be set apart and devoted to God. To be holy means to be different in every aspect of our lives and behavior, in our conversation and in our thinking. We are to be pure and holy. We are not to be tainted or contaminated. Let your minds be filled with what is true, honorable, upright, and pure, or else take and focus on what is false, shameful, immoral, and tainted.

Everything We Love

Paul then tells us to let our minds be filled with love, with everything we love. This means what is worthy of love, what calls forth and elicits love, what is lovable. This was one of the main qualities that children and adults alike saw and met in Jesus. He was full of grace, truth, and love. He was winsome and attractive, worth loving and being attached to. He was charming. This was not what we detest and find hateful. We are to let our minds be filled with everything that we love and admire.

Whatever Is Good

Paul urges us to let our minds be filled with what we admire, what is of good report, what is fair sounding, well spoken of, and what is clearly admirable and worthy of admiration. This is not what we all know and disapprove of or what is negative and unworthy. Let our minds be filled with whatever is good. This is what is full of virtue and what is excellent.

To those who ask, "What do you mean and how do we know what it is?" we may reply, "We know it when we see it. We know it when we meet it. We know it when we read it. We know it when we watch it. We know it when we hear it."

Consider music. Karl Barth used to say that God listens to Bach, but when the angels play, they listen to Mozart. We recognize the excellence in Bach and Mozart. If we look at the ceiling of the Sistine Chapel or at Michelangelo's statue of David, we see and know excellence. When we read the Scriptures, contemplate the heavens, or hear of heroism and bravery, we recognize what is good and full of virtue.

After the terrible Tube and Bus bombings on a Thursday in London, the very next Saturday one quarter of a million people filled the Mall outside Buckingham Palace in celebration of VE and VJ Day. But it was more than just an honoring of the sacrifice of many and the victory of the Allies. It was a brave refusal of Londoners and the British people to allow terrorism to win or cow them into cowardly submission. It was a clear example of heroism, bravery, and what is good expressed practically in the face of and in response to evil.

We are to fill our minds with what is not bad, not evil, not poor, and not second rate. We are to fill our minds with what is praiseworthy and worthy of praise, not with things worthy of blame. We are to fill our minds with things worth shouting about, worth celebrating, worth proclaiming, worth talking about, preaching about, gossiping about, and sharing.

"So finally brothers and sisters, whatever is true, whatever is noble, whatever is pure, whatever is lovely, whatever is admirable—anything and everything that is excellent and praiseworthy, then think about such things." Fill your minds with them. Whatever you have learned or received or heard from the apostle Paul or seen in him, then put them into practice. And so the God of peace will be with you.

Oxford teaching is wonderful. It is a very simple system that has lasted since the 1170s. It was used by Lewis and is still used today. The reason it is wonderful is that the student does all the work and the don/tutor takes all the credit. We call this the tutorial system. Each student is given a topic every week in term. The student departs to spend a week reading, researching, crafting an essay, and then comes along a week later to the tutorial and reads the essay aloud to the tutor. You, the tutor, listen and politely say, "Thank you." We always accentuate the positive just before we put the boot in. Then in a gentle, loving way you tear the essay apart line by line, in terms of its structure, content, argument, conclusion, and application. Then you indicate to the student how to improve and produce a better essay. This is slightly better than the infamous tutor who listened to an essay and commented, "You could take that essay and tear it in half and throw half of it away. And it wouldn't matter which half." Instead you send them away with another topic for another essay the following week. We do this for eight weeks. This is as long as we can stand the students. This is what we do, and we call it teaching!

Having taught in Oxford for twenty-six years, I have devised one question I ask every student at the end of every tutorial, whether a graduate or undergraduate: "So what?"

It is a good question for us today. This is the beginning of the C. S. Lewis Oxford and Cambridge conference: "So what?"

For us, as we go back to our home settings and contexts, work, vocations, settings, and roles, "So what?" For us in the battle of good versus evil, "So what?" So, how do we fill our minds with these qualities? Remember the title of the conference: "Making All Things New: The Good, the True, and the Beautiful in the Twenty-first Century." We have a choice. We can settle for evil or for making all things new. But how? So what are we to do?

We Need a Right View of God

We need to remember that this is God's work and not just ours. It belongs to God and not to us. All we do depends on God and not on us. It is God's grace that is more than sufficient. To be able to fill our minds with what really matters depends on the power and love of God. He is able to do exceedingly abundantly above all that we ask or think. God's nature is not just love, power, and grace. God is the One who makes all things new—a transforming God. He is the One who saves, restores, redeems, satisfies, purifies, and inspires. We need a right view of God who makes all things new. So let Him!

We Need a Right View of Ourselves

It does not all depend on me or us. Christian living and the Christian life is not a do-it-yourself or a do-it-together religion. It is being able to do it in the power of the Holy Spirit. Living the Christian life is not just trying to follow the example of Jesus Christ. It is living in the power of Christ and the power of his Holy Spirit. The Spirit is the Comforter, the one who inspires us, supports and enables us, and fills us. He is the One Who leads us into all truth. It does not all depend on us, however. We are also coworkers with God. We are part, and an integral part, of God's plan of salvation, redemption, and restoration. We are part of making all things new in science, literature, social and political life, preaching, praying, evangelism, and our life together. We are making all things new with God. He is able and enables us so to do.

We Need a Right View of the Future

I love the poster with the legend, "Please be patient with me. God hasn't finished with me yet." Please be patient with the state of the world; God has not finished yet. Please be patient in the struggle between good and evil; God has not finished yet. This is not an argument or plea to be complacent. It is rather to ensure that we do actually have a right view, in which God is recognized as being in ultimate control. We must realize that God has all power, love, and grace. That God is the One who inspires and enables. That God calls us to work with Him as He makes all things new.

There will come a time when the lion lies down with the lamb, when swords will be turned into plows and spears into pruning hooks. There will come a time when people from every tribe and every nation will gather not in a garden as in the beginning, but in a city where God himself is at the center of all things. The dwelling of God will be with humanity. There will be no more death, mourning, crying, or pain, for the old order will have passed away and all things made new. Nothing impure, no one who does what is shameful and deceitful, will be there. Only those whose names are written in the Lamb's book of life will be gathered there. The nations will be healed. We shall serve Him and see His face. There will be no more night, nor the need for light from lamps or the sun, for the Lord our God will give us light, and He shall reign for ever and ever.

All things will be made new. But for now, finally, my brothers and sisters, in the struggle between good and evil and in the choice between good and evil, let your minds be filled with everything that is true, everything that is honorable, everything that is upright and pure, everything that we love and admire, with whatever is good and praiseworthy. In God's name, and in the power of God with God's help, we, with God, can make all things new (Phil. 4:8).

Disaffections

Like a young child squirming
    to escape the embrace and kisses
    of a loving grandmother,
we rush through our prayers,
    our minds moving on to something else,
but still she keeps an eye on us
    and tucks us in
    at night.

Jackson, Tenn.
April 7, 2004

On Being Glad for the Good

Ben Patterson

TEXTS: 1 Peter 1:8–9; Psalm 118:1–4

Sunday dinner at my Grandma's house was always a memorable event. Food appeared on the massive oak table like royalty in a court. King Roast Beef sat at one end of the table, Queen Mashed Potatoes at the other end, with Sir Gravy at her side, surrounded splendiferously by the rest of the court: fresh garden corn and tomatoes, home baked bread, scallions and green peas and raspberry jam and ice cold milk and tea. Out of sight, but not smell, the hot apple pie waited in state to be unveiled at the end. Okay, I'm overreaching. But you must understand—I really loved Sunday dinner at Grandma's house. It was an occasion of reverence and joy.

The most memorable of these memorable meals happened when I was about eight years old. Since I especially loved the mashed potatoes and gravy part, I always tried to position myself at the seat near them. So on this particular day I sat with the vatlike bowl of mashed potatoes right in front of my face, almost exactly at eye level. Steam rose from the mountain of potatoes; butter ran in rivers down its canyons. As people were gathering around the table, I was thinking of how I would do the gravy.

Should I build a little potato castle in the middle, with a moat for the gravy around it? Or should I make a giant lake in the middle? I decided on the lake.

When everyone was seated, my Grandpa asked Uncle Albert to pray. That's not his name, but I'll use the alias to…you'll see why. Uncle Albert was an odd man from a part of the family some of us were a little uncomfortable with. I don't remember which church they went to, but I once heard the word "holy rollers" whispered in reference to them. I didn't know what that meant; but since it was whispered, I was hesitant to ask what the strange phrase meant. I found out when he started to give thanks for the food. Albert prayed with great feeling and volume. He was truly grateful for the food. So was I. But he was grateful in detail. He thanked God for the scallions and the peas and the beef. He rhapsodized over the plates and forks and knives. He sang of Grandma and the "hands that prepared" the food. He extolled the name of God for his wonderful generosity. He wept and clapped his hands for joy. I began to notice the steam wasn't rising as high on the mashed potatoes as it was when his interminable prayer began. My heart sank as his rose, and the potatoes grew cold.

I was disgusted when he finished and resented for years what he did, but the seed of a new idea was planted in my mind: joy is what you experience when you are grateful for the grace that has been given you. Indeed, if one could ever take truly to heart the goodness and generosity of God—really see it in its height, depth, width, and length[1]—one might act just like my uncle Albert. If our gratitude could perfectly correspond to the grace that is given us, then no amount of thanksgiving and joy could possibly be excessive. Gratitude and joy are the twin children of grace, organically joined, theologically and spiritually.

In the Greek language, they are even related linguistically. The words for grace, gratitude, and joy all have the same root,

[1]See Ephesians 3:14–21.

char, a noun that refers to health and well-being. Grace is *charis,* gratitude is *eucharistia,* and joy is *chara.*

What is merely pictured in Greek is a burning reality in the kingdom of God. Grace is God's mercy, his unmerited favor. It is what Frederick Buechner calls the "crucial eccentricity" of the Christian faith, the unique and wonderfully odd thing God does to forgive sinners: not giving them the bad things they deserve, but rather giving them the incredibly good things they don't deserve. The great gospel mystery is not that bad things sometimes happen to good people, but that such a good and gracious thing has happened to bad people, guilty and broken people, who have discovered God's amazing love to be that "while we were still sinners, Christ died for us" (Rom. 5:8b, NIV).

What else can one be but grateful when that happens? "How can anything more or different be asked of man?" asks Karl Barth. "The only answer to charis is eucharistia… Grace and gratitude belong together like heaven and earth. Grace evokes gratitude like the voice of an echo. Gratitude follows grace like thunder lightning."[2] And as gratitude follows grace, so joy follows gratitude, for joy is what one feels when truly and hugely grateful.

The pattern runs throughout scripture: God does something wonderful, and people praise and thank him, joyfully. What else could they do, praise him somberly? Praise him apathetically? Praise him morosely? Of course the very idea is ridiculous, oxymoronic. Genuine gratitude must necessarily also be joyful. The greater the grace, the greater the gratitude; the greater the gratitude, the greater the joy.

Psalm 95, for instance, begins with a call to be grateful and joyful in a big way:

"Come, let us sing for joy to the LORD; / let us shout aloud to the Rock of our salvation. / Let us come before him with thanksgiving / and extol him with music and song." Why such exuberance? Because God is just very, extremely super-outstanding, that's why: "For the Lord is the great God, / the

---

[2]Karl Barth, *Church Dogmatics,* ed. G. W. Bromiley and T. F. Torrance, trans. G. W. Bromiley, "The Doctrine of Reconciliation," IV.1 (Edinburgh: T. and T. Clark, 1980), 41.

great King above all gods. / In his hand are the depths of the earth, / and the mountain peaks belong to him. / The sea is his, for he made it, / and his hands formed the dry land" (vv. 1–5, NIV).

That is reason enough to be very grateful and joyful. But there is more: Not only is God beyond impressive in his creative power, but he has taken a special liking to us. He is intimately involved in our well-being: "For he is our God/ and we are the people of his pasture, / the flock under his care" (v. 7, NIV). The joy of genuine gratitude follows grace like thunder follows lightning.

There is a spirituality, a kind of piety to a gathering like this Oxbridge. Our theme is: "Making All Things New: The Good, the True, and the Beautiful in the Twenty-first Century." The spirituality is: goodness, truth, and beauty evoke gratitude like the voice of an echo. Gratitude follows grace like thunder lightning. In the same way, *God's goodness is something to be glad about, as is his truth and his beauty. Being glad in the good is the spirituality.*

Whatever else we do, let us be glad in the good, happy in the true, and let us rejoice in the beautiful! The good, the true, and the beautiful are more than great ideas; they are words that speak of the character of God and his gracious deeds on our behalf. They call for the worship of this great God.

The Christian doesn't start with ideas—the Christian starts with the God who gives the ideas. Mere ideas move us to reflection and thought. God moves us to that and more. God moves us to worship. When David, the activist king, considered God's goodness to him in protecting him from his enemies, he prayed that he might become a contemplative and worship God forever! "One thing I ask of the LORD, / this is what I seek: / that I may dwell in the house of the LORD / all the days of my life, / to gaze upon the beauty of the LORD / and to seek him in his temple" (Ps. 27:4, NIV).

The praise of the God who is good, true, and beautiful moves us to do good, true, and beautiful things. Consider the woman with the jar of expensive perfume. She did the grossly inappropriate: she crossed social and gender barriers to enter an all-male gathering. Though unwelcome there, she nevertheless opened the jar and poured a fragrant, high-priced perfume on Jesus' head.

When some of the men began to mutter about how inappropriate it was, how the perfume cost the equivalent of a year's wages, and how all that money could have been better spent on the poor, Jesus spoke forcefully: "Leave her alone…Why are you bothering her? She has done a beautiful thing to me" (Mk. 14:6, NIV). The Greek word translated "beautiful" is *kalos,* meaning "fine," "beautiful," "elegant." It was used in the Septuagint, the Greek Old Testament, to describe what pleases God, what gives him joy. Jesus thus judged her "excess" as entirely appropriate, and said of it something he said of no other human act: "I tell you the truth, wherever the gospel is preached throughout the world, what she has done will also be told, in memory of her" (Mk. 14:9, NIV). And indeed it has been told, countless times in every corner of the earth.

That's how highly God regards this kind of joyful gratitude. In language that echoes the words of communion, "do this in my memory," he blessed the expression of her gratitude as corresponding perfectly to the grace that had been given her, and therefore worthy of universal remembrance. The woman's act of extravagant worship was a simple outpouring of good for Good, true for True, beautiful for Beautiful.

Spiritualities have disciplines: Ours should be to practice gratitude and pursue joy; to worship God not only *because* we understand something about him, but *in order that* we may understand something about him. Let us be glad in the good and rejoice in the true and beautiful because gratitude and joy are organs of perception; we don't see in order to give thanks and rejoice, we give thanks and rejoice in order to see. Our perceptions are radically the result of our dispositions. Virginia Owens writes:

> For if you go poking about the world, intent on keeping the candle of consciousness blazing, you must be ready to

give thanks at all times. Discrimination is not allowed. The flame cannot gutter and fail when a cold wind whistles throughout the house. Thanksgiving, thanksgiving. All must be thanksgiving…Thanksgiving is not a task to be taken lightly. It is not for dilettantes or aesthetes. One does not dabble in praise for one's own amusement, nor train the intellect and develop perceptual skills to add to his repertoire. We are not thinking about the world as a free course in art appreciation. No. Thanksgiving is not the result of perception; thanksgiving is the access to perception.[3]

I think it works this way: At the end of Dante's *Divine Comedy*, after he has gone through hell and purgatory, in heaven he is finally led into the very presence of God to gaze into the face of God. The effect this vision has on him is the kind of thing the theme of this conference should have on us all. He wrote: "But now my desire and will were revolved, like a wheel which is moved evenly, by the Love which moves the sun and other stars" (Canto 33, "Paradiso").[4]

That is what this gathering is all about: that our desires and wills be moved by the same love that moves the sun and other stars. That, I submit, is a more elegant version of Uncle Albert at Sunday dinner. There is a feast spread out before us at this conference, but the feast is just the hors d'oeuvres of an eternity with God. God is the ultimate Feast. "Both high and low among men / find refuge in the shadow of your wings. / They feast on the abundance of your house; / you give them drink from your river of delights. / For with you is the fountain of life; / in your light we see light" (Ps. 36:7b—9, NIV).

Glory be to the Father, and to the Son, and to the Holy Spirit. As it was in the beginning, is now, and ever will be, unto the ages of the ages. Amen.

---

[3]Virginia Stem Owens, *And the Trees Clap Their Hands* (Grand Rapids: Eerdmans, 1983), quoted in Bob Benson and Michael W. Benson, *Disciplines for the Inner Life* (Waco, Tex.: Word Books, 1985), 334.

[4]*The Divine Comedy of Dante Alighieri,* trans. Charles Eliot Norton (Chicago: The Great Books of the Western World, Encyclopedia Britannica, 1952), 157.

Anastasia

Wrinkles and decay
wash away
like dirt at the end of the day.
Years disappear
with sorrow and tear
when the grave poses no fear.
As mourning turns to morning
when the dead seed sprouts
the shriveled kernel awakens:
a tree of life!

Jackson, Tenn.
May 2004

We Will Be Like Him

Frederica Mathewes-Green

TEXT: 1 John 3:2

England can be delightful in early August, when the mornings are cool and the afternoons bright. At home, on America's mid-Atlantic coast, it's so hot and gummy that the dogs are sticking to the sidewalks. This is one of those rare patches of year when Americans might like to come to England for the weather.

Yet in the Holy Land it's hotter still, as any pilgrim can tell you. This year's Oxbridge conference concludes on the feast of the Transfiguration, that event that arises from the most somnolent point of summer, when August is a still lake of heat. If you have been to the Holy Land during such seasons, you know that the sun beats down relentlessly, and the shrubs turn gray and dusty. Everywhere you look there is rock and rubble. It was on August 6, as the church remembers, that Jesus took his closest disciples, Peter and James and John, and led them up the side of "a high mountain." Mount Tabor claims this honor.

This is how Matthew tells the story:

> After six days Jesus took with him Peter and James and John his brother, and led them up a high mountain

23

apart. And he was transfigured before them, and his face shone like the sun, and his garments became as white as light. And behold, there appeared to them Moses and Elijah, talking with him. And Peter said to Jesus, "Lord, it is well that we are here; if you wish, I will make three booths here, one for you and one for Moses and one for Elijah." He was still speaking, when lo, a bright cloud overshadowed them, and a voice from the cloud said, "This is my beloved Son, with whom I am well pleased; listen to him." When the disciples heard this, they fell on their faces, and were filled with awe. But Jesus came and touched them, saying, "Rise, and have no fear." And when they lifted up their eyes, they saw no one but Jesus only. (Mt. 17:1—8, RSV)

Perhaps these three disciples were used to being taken aside for private conferences. But they were not prepared for what happened that day. They saw Jesus "transfigured before them, and his face shone like the sun." They saw Moses and Elijah speaking with him. Peter then began to babble the first excited thing that popped into his head. That was when the bright cloud overshadowed them, and they heard the Father's voice. No wonder they tumbled to the ground in awe. Then when Jesus came and touched them, saying, "Have no fear," they looked up to find they were alone.

In the Sinai desert, a bit south of Mount Tabor, on the slopes of Mount Sinai itself, a monastery has stood for fifteen hundred years. Long before its walls were built, the place was already a site of pilgrimage, where men and women withdrew to those desolate crags to live lives of intense and dedicated prayer. We know them as the Desert Fathers and Mothers. Because Bedouin marauders threatened their lives, in the sixth century the Emperor Justinian built a sturdy monastery to protect the Christians there.

In this monastery of St. Catherine, on Mount Sinai, is a church. In the church, in the curved apse above the altar, is a mosaic depiction of the Transfiguration. Since our conference focuses so much on beauty, it is a good time to appreciate the way that earlier generations of believers honored their Lord in the visual arts. These early images are, of course, called "icons," the Greek word for "image." In the centuries when most people were illiterate, when Bibles were extremely expensive and rare, the most accessible "Bible" would be illustrations such as this. Worshipers would hear a part of the Scripture cycle read during services every week, but all during the year they could study the figures on the walls and ceilings of churches and recall the truths that they depict. Unfortunately, very few early icons survive, because they were destroyed during the "Iconoclast Controversy" in the eighth century. This Transfiguration on the ceiling of the Sinai monastery church was spared simply because the location is so remote.

This icon is dominated by a magnificent standing image of Christ, transfigured in glory. Elijah stands in midair on the left and Moses on the right, both in stances that suggest lively conversation. Below them, along the bottom edge, we see John on the left—that is, on Christ's right hand—falling to his knees with his hands raised in prayer. John's brother James, on the right, also kneels and seems to cower before the weight of the event. Beneath the feet of Christ, Peter has fallen prostrate. A moment before this, he had been sputtering about building booths for the three holy figures to occupy.

This image is more astonishing than it initially looks, because it is not painted but is a mosaic. Thousands of tiny chips of stone and colored glass, called *tesserae,* combine to create the picture. It is more difficult to make an image this way, and the flowing movement a paintbrush so easily captures can be hard to achieve unless the tesserae are very tiny.

Yet mosaics have the advantage of being nearly impervious to time. As long as they stick to the wall, their color will not dim; and they can be cleaned of the smoke of incense and oil lamps without damaging the underlying image. The glass gives off a shimmering light, especially when the tesserae are set to reflect at subtly different angles, as in the gold background of this icon.

Something more about the artist's work deserves appreciation. When you look at a photograph of this icon it appears flat, but in fact it is applied to the conch of the sanctuary apse, a curved half-shell. This is quite an achievement. It is difficult to design an icon for a dome, because the concave surface tends to throw elements out of proportion; things at the outer edge appear to be huge, while those in the high center look tiny. The artists responsible for this mosaic compensated for the curve so skillfully that when viewed directly the bowl of the apse is imperceptible. This debunks the idea that early Christian artists knew nothing about perspective. On the contrary, perspective is sometimes intentionally distorted in icons to convey a sense of being outside predictable space, or of the image pressing or rushing out toward the viewer—techniques not used again until the Cubists. The making of icons was (and still is) considered an act of worship. The artists who designed and installed this image would have made it with prayer and fasting, hoping to impart to viewers some of the same awe and love that Peter, James, and John felt.

Christ gazes out steadily, bearing authority and love. White rays streak out from the sides of his dark blue *mandorla,* an oval space that seems to recede back into eternity, to the foundation of the universe. Christ is truly the center—of this image, of everything: "He is the image of the invisible God, the first-born of all creation; for in him all things were created, in heaven and on earth, visible and invisible, whether thrones or dominions or principalities or authorities—all things were created through him and for him. He is before all things, and in him all things hold together" (Col. 1:15—17, RSV).

But the main thing about the story of the Transfiguration is that Christ is glowing. He is turning into light. What can we make of a story like this? What did Peter and John make of it? It seems, understandably, to have made an indelible impression. In his second letter, Peter retells the story, preceding it with this assurance: "We were eyewitnesses of his majesty" (2 Pet. 1:16b, RSV). John begins his intricately woven first letter with a similar eyewitness claim: "That which was from the beginning, which we have heard, which we have seen with our eyes" (John 1:1a). John continues, "This is the message we have heard from him and proclaim to you, that God is light and in him is no darkness at all" (v. 5, RSV).

God is light. Throughout the Scriptures, God appears repeatedly in the form of overwhelming light. A cloud covers the mountaintop when Christ's glory is revealed, just as one shook Mount Sinai with lightning when Moses spoke with God. When Moses descended the mountain carrying the tablets of the Law, his face was shining from the presence of God: "The Israelites could not look on Moses' face because of its brightness" (2 Cor. 3:7b, RSV). Pillars of cloud and of fire led the Israelites in the wilderness. Paul on the road to Damascus was overwhelmed by "a light from heaven, brighter than the sun" (Acts 26:13b, RSV).

But there is something about light that most previous generations would have known, but that does not occur to us today. We think of light as something you get with the flip of a switch. However, until a hundred years ago, light always meant fire. Whether it was the flame of a candle, an oil lamp, a campfire, or the blazing noonday sun, light was always accompanied by fire. Fire, as everyone knew, must be respected. That is one of the lessons learned from earliest childhood. Fire is powerful and dangerous. It does not compromise. In any confrontation, it is the person who will be changed by fire, and not the other way round. As Hebrews 12:29 says, "Our God is a consuming fire" (RSV).

Yet this consuming fire was something God's people yearned for. In some mysterious way, light means life. John tells us, "In him was life, and the life was the light of men" (Jn. 1:4). Jesus says, "I am...the life" (Jn. 11:25, RSV), and also, "I am the light" (Jn. 8:12).

Light is life: we live in light, and could not live without it. In some sense, we live *on* light. It is light-energy that plants consume in photosynthesis—an everyday miracle as mysterious as life itself. When we eat plants, or eat the animals that eat plants, we feed second-hand on light. Light is converted into life, literally, with every bite we eat.

The fire of God consumes us, and we consume it as well. His light is life. "Truly, truly, I say to you, unless you eat the flesh of the Son of man and drink his blood, you have no life in you" (Jn. 6:53). What could Jesus have meant by this? In recent centuries, Western Christians have offered competing theories. Some hold that Jesus meant a memorial meal, a simple commemoration of his sacrifice; but the Greek text of John's gospel makes a literal interpretation inescapable, for there Jesus uses the most offensive terms possible. He did not use the ordinary word for "eat" (*phago*), but *trogo,* to munch and chew as a cow chews its cud. He did not even refer to his body (*soma*), but to his flesh (*sarx*). "Chew my flesh"—he could not have made it much more graphic. Jesus' intended audience obviously took it this way: they were appalled. John tells us that "many" of Jesus' disciples abandoned him because of this "hard saying." When Jesus asks the twelve whether they, too, will leave, Peter hardly sounds enthusiastic. But stalwart resignation speaks: "Lord, to whom shall we go?" (v. 58).

On the far side of everything—the Last Supper, the campfire denial, the Resurrection, and the Pentecost outpouring—Peter tries in a letter to make sense of what happened on Mount Tabor that day. Peter saw God's glory, and he knows it is for us. He says that God's divine power calls us "to his own glory." Through his promises we may "become partakers of the divine nature" (2 Pet. 1:3—4, RSV).

"Partakers of the divine nature"—The life that is in Christ will be in us. In Western Christianity, we tend to take scriptures like this metaphorically. When Paul refers to life "in Christ" some 140 times, we expect he means a life that *looks like* Christ's life. We try to imitate our Lord, and sing of following him and seeking his will. We ask, "What would Jesus do?" We hope to behave ethically and fairly in this life, and after death take up citizenship in heaven.

But it appears that Peter had learned to anticipate something more radical and more intimate: true oneness with Christ and personal transfiguration. We partake of, consume, the light of Tabor and the life of Christ. We receive not mere intellectual knowledge of God, but illumination. This participation in "the divine nature" is not a treat squirreled away for the select few, for mystics or hobbyists of "spiritual formation," but God's plan for every single human life: "The true light that enlightens every man was coming into the world" (Jn. 1:9, RSV). Participation in this light is not a lofty or esoteric path, but one of simplicity and childlike humility. It is not enjoyed in sudden, swooping supernatural experiences, but gained by daily, diligent self-control. Through prayer, fasting, and honoring others above self, we gradually clear away everything in us that will not catch fire.

We are made to catch fire. We are like lumps of coal, dusty and inert, and possess little of which to be proud; but we have one talent: we can burn. You could say that it is our destiny to burn. God made us that way, because he intended for his blazing light to fill us. When this happens, "your whole body will be full of light" (Mt. 6:22, RSV): our bodies, not just our souls. Just as Jesus' body on Mount Tabor was radiant with the glory of God, our bodies will "bear the image of the man of heaven" (1 Cor. 15:49, RSV). This very same too-familiar body, that embarrasses and disappoints, that is marred by flaws and flab, will one day be "raised in glory" (1 Cor. 15:43, RSV). As Cyril of Alexandria wrote in the fifth century, "Even though [the disciples had] heard that our flesh would rise up again, they did not know how. Now [Christ] was transfigured in his own flesh, and so gave us the example."[1] And as John, another witness of Mount Tabor, writes: "It does not yet appear what we shall be, but we know that when he appears we shall be like him" (1 John 3:2, RSV).

---

[1]Quoted in Michele Piccirillo, "The Mountain of the Transfiguration," available online at http://198.62.75.1/www1/ofm/san/TAB05mnt.html.

Even the astonishing glory that Peter and James and John saw on the mountain was not all the glory that God is. In the Orthodox Church, we sing an ancient hymn on the feast of the Transfiguration that begins:

> Thou wast transfigured on the mount, O Christ our
> God,
> Revealing thy glory to thy disciples as far as they
> could bear it.

What they saw was only the amount that they could bear, carefully adjusted to their capacity by a loving God. The glimpse they had of transformation, they believed, is what God intended for them as well.

It is easy to forget this. C. S. Lewis's literary demon, Screwtape, was able to get a man's mind off hair-raising spiritual realities just by showing him a shouting newsboy and a passing city bus. We are grateful for distractions because, if the gospel of Jesus is true, we will have to change our lives. If God's plan is to fill our souls and bodies with his brilliant life, we must decide whether we will cooperate. If we do, we will have to train ourselves to "pray without ceasing" (1 Thess. 5:17, KJV), gazing constantly on God who dwells in our hearts, "as the eyes of servants / look to the hand of their master" (Ps. 123:2a, RSV). We will have to start remembering that every other human being we encounter, no matter how exasperating, is a recipient of this same divine invitation; every person we meet is called to blaze up with glory. The fear and trembling that seized Peter, James, and John on the mountain will accompany our every remembrance of God, driving out triviality and self-satisfaction. We supply the coal; God supplies the fire: "Work out your own salvation with fear and trembling; for God is at work in you" (Phil. 2:12, RSV).

Where are we going? We're all going up Mount Tabor. "And we all, with unveiled face, beholding the glory of the Lord, are being changed into his likeness from one degree of glory to another" (2 Cor. 3:18, RSV).

Leadership

Part of the circle,
a seat at the table,
in the game;
learning to play
the mutual admiration ritual—
not to make a difference
but to receive invitations,
like an admiral in the tsar's navy,
all brocade and silk
while confusing them
for something that matters.

Saint Valentine's Day 1998
Jackson, Tenn.

4

The Good, the True, and the Beautiful

To What Purpose?

Rick Warren

TEXT: Colossians 1:16

I have been given the subject of "The Good, the True, and the Beautiful: To What Purpose?" That means I could go anywhere with this talk. We could spend about a month just on what is goodness, what is truth, what is beauty. I assume I am here for that last one: purpose. As I thought about this subject, I was reminded of one of my favorite C. S. Lewis quotes. He said, "If I find in myself a desire which no experience in this world can satisfy, the most probable explanation is that I was made for another world."[1] That, my friends, is the purpose driven life. If you want to know the purpose of life in a nutshell, I will give it to you in three words: preparation for eternity. We were not made for time; we were made for eternity. The Bible says that

---

[1]C. S. Lewis, *Mere Christianity* (New York: HarperSanFrancisco, 2001), 136–37.

you were made in God's image, and that means you are not an animal. You are a soul. You are given the ability to create, and you are given the ability to communicate with God: to know and love him as much as he knows and loves you. It also means that you were made to last forever. One day your heart is going to stop, and that will be the end of the body; but that will not be the end of you, because you were made to last forever. That means you are going to spend far more time on the other side of death than you do on this side. On this side of death, you will get to sixty, eighty, at the most a hundred years. On the other side of death you will live trillions, and trillions, and trillions, and trillions, and trillions of years. So the big question then becomes, "What on earth am I here for?" If I only get a hundred years here, at the most, and trillions of years on the other side of death, what am I here for?

I think there are three fundamental questions in life. There is the question of existence: why am I alive? There is the question of intention: what is my purpose? There is the question of significance: does my life matter? I have traveled around the world. I have trained about 400,000 pastors in about 160 countries. In these travels I have learned that these are the universal questions. It does not matter how poor or rich you are, how educated or uneducated you are, everybody at some point in their life puts their head down on the pillow and says: what is it all about, Alfie? What am I here for? What is my purpose? What is life all about? Does my life matter? And people care about these questions.

This last year my life has been so varied. Last week I was working in an AIDS hospice in Rwanda. I lectured at Harvard a couple months before and at the University of Judaism, places like that. I have seen all sides of society. From business leaders in the White House to everyday people like you and me, everyone has these questions. What is my purpose? What is the meaning of my life? We may well explore "The Good, the True, and the Beautiful: To What Purpose?"

The truth is that God has never created anything without a purpose. Every rock has a purpose, every plant has a purpose, every animal has a purpose, every tree has a purpose. God does not create anything without a purpose! That means if your heart is still beating right now, then God has a purpose for your life. Now here is the problem: if you want to know the purpose of life, where do you look? If I were to hold up an invention right now—an invention you had never seen—and said, "What is the purpose of this invention?" you would not have the slightest idea what its purpose was because you had never seen it. The only way you could know its purpose would be (a) talk to the inventor who created it, or (b) read the owner's manual. The same is true for your life.

The only way you are going to know the purpose for your life is to either talk to your Creator or read the owner's manual. You see, there are really only two ways to discover the purpose of life. The first way is simply speculation. You can take a philosophy course, put on a cardigan, get your latte and your pipe, and sit in Starbucks and say: "Why am I here? Where are we going? What is my purpose?" The truth is that philosophy has tremendous value for our lives. When it comes to the purpose of life, however, even the best of philosophers are just speculating. They are guessing.

The only way you can know the purpose of life is not through speculation but through revelation. Some of you— many of you—are from America, and you know there is the spiritualization/Oprah Winfrey approach to finding your purpose. The big popular way to finding your purpose in America, and even around the world, is this: they say, "If you want to know your purpose, then look within." It is kind of like, "Trust the force, Luke." Look within. Well, I looked within, and I did not like what I saw. I just got more confused. Somebody needs to stand up and say that the king is not wearing any clothes.

For years we have been told to look within to discover the purpose of life. There is only one problem with that: it does not work! If you could discover your purpose by looking within yourself, then everybody would know his or her purpose. We have all looked within at different times. The truth is that you did not create you, so you cannot tell you why you exist. Only the Creator knows the reason for the creation, and the Bible says we are made to last forever.

Psalm 119:19 says that I am here on earth for just a little while. Psalm 33:11 says that God's plans endure forever, and his purposes last eternally. That means God has long-range plans for you. God's purposes for your life extend much further than the sixty, eighty, or one hundred years that you will live on this planet—because God's purposes, the Scriptures say, are eternal: they last forever!

I love *The Message* paraphrase of Colossians 1:16, which says, "For everything, absolutely everything, above and below, visible and invisible . . . *everything* got started in him and finds its purpose in him." We find our purpose in Christ, and we find our purpose in our Creator who *is* Christ. Therefore, life is preparation for eternity, and as I read scripture, I find that this is the warm-up act to the real show. This is the dress rehearsal before the real play begins. This is the preschool, this is the kindergarten, and this is the first lap around the race before the real race begins in eternity. This is the "get ready" stage.

When you get to heaven, you are going to do certain things. You are going to worship God. We know that. You are going to fellowship with other believers. We know that. You are going to grow and become like Christ; we shall see him as he is, and we shall become like him. You are going to serve him. So what does God want you to do while you are here on earth? It is simple: *practice*! He wants you to practice doing on earth what you are going to be doing for all eternity so that when you get to heaven you will not look like a "dufus."

Planned for God's Pleasure: Worship

The Bible tells us very clearly throughout all of Scripture that you were planned for God's pleasure. You were created for God's pleasure: that is called worship. The Bible tells us that you were formed for God's family: that is called fellowship. And the Bible tells us in Romans 8:29 and other passages that you were created to become like Christ: that is discipleship. The Bible tells us that you were shaped to serve God, wired in the ways of service: that is ministry. The Bible tells us that you were made for a mission: that is evangelism. It is interesting, but of those four, the only one you cannot do in heaven is evangelism. You can worship, fellowship, grow, serve, relax, have fun, eat—there are only two things you cannot do in heaven. Have you ever figured this out? One of them is sin, and the other is witness. Which of those two do you think God leaves you here on earth to do? You cannot witness in heaven because there are not any unbelievers there! Have you ever thought about this: why does God not just kill you the moment you step across the line into a covenant relationship with him and are born again and you put your trust in him? Why does God not just instantly zap you and take you to heaven? Because he wants you to practice some things here on earth. Once you are in, why does he let us handle all of the trials and tribulations and problems? Or the good things: the good, the true, and the beautiful? Let us just look at these for a minute.

You are planned for God's pleasure. The Bible tells us in Revelation 4:11 that God created everything and it is for his pleasure that they exist. Psalm 149:4 says, "For the LORD takes pleasure in His people" (NKJV). Let me ask you a question. How many of you are parents? Do you take pleasure in your kids? And you say, "Most of the time!" God takes pleasure in us most of the time. When my kids were little—I have three children and some grandchildren, now—they did not have to be doing anything spiritual for me to be taking pleasure in them. They did not have to be witnessing, they did not have to be reading the Bible, they did not have to be praying, they did not have to come up to me and say, "Hey Dad, here is the latest verse I memorized." I just enjoyed watching them be them! In fact, when my kids were little I used to go into their rooms at night, and I would sit on the edge of their beds and watch their chests rise and fall. I would watch them breathe. I would watch their little chests go up and down, up and down, up and down. That gave me so much pleasure because *I* was their father! They did not have to be doing anything fantastic, I just *loved* them!

Did you know that God takes pleasure in watching you sleep? Have you ever thought about that? Have you ever thought about the fact that God takes pleasure in looking down and watching you be you? "That's my girl. That's my boy. They are doing human things, the things I made them to do." God takes pleasure in all of that. You see, the Bible says that God is love. It does not say that God *has* love; it says he *is* love. It is the essence of his nature, it is his character, it is his being: God *is* love. The Bible also says that you and I were created as objects of God's love. If you want to know the whole reason you are sitting there right now with your heart beating, it is because God made you to love you. That is the whole reason you are alive! If God had not wanted to love you, *you* would not be living. The Bible says you were created as an object of God's love.

Now, God was not lonely. God has never been *lonely*. He exists in the Trinity in perfect fellowship. He is love himself. He did not *need* us; he *wanted* us. The Bible teaches us that the entire universe was created so that the earth could exist so that the human race could exist so that you could exist so that God could love you. Now let me tell you something: if you are a believer, if you have been in church all your life, then you have heard all your life that "God loves you." It just rolls off your back. But I have met people who have been believers for fifty or sixty years that have never *felt* it. It is just a mind thing: they have never felt love. If you ever get what I have just told you—and you get it at the depth of your emotion where you understand that God created the universe so he could create you so he could love you, and you were made as an object of his love and as an object of his pleasure, and God gets pleasure out of watching you be you—then you will never have to deal with inferiority or insecurity or self worth, when you realize that you matter to God!

Do you want to know how much you matter to God? Look at the cross! Jesus stretched out his nail-pierced hands and said, "*This* much! *This* is how much I love you! I love you so much it hurts! I would rather *die* than live without you! I love you this much." That the God of the universe would come to earth and die on a cross for me is absolutely mind-boggling. We were created for God's pleasure.

In Hosea 6:6, God says that *I do not want your sacrifice; I want your love. I do not want your offerings; I want you to know me.* Do you hear the longing of our Creator in that? He says, "You know what? I want you to *know* and *love* me." The greatest thing you can know in life is that you were created to be loved by God, and the greatest thing you can do back is learn to love him back. That is why Jesus is walking down the street one day when a guy walks up and says to him, "Okay, Lord, I need to know shorthand for the Bible. Summarize it for me. Tell me what matters most!" And Jesus says, "Okay, I'll summarize it for you. All the Law and the Prophets right here: *Cliff's Notes* on the Old Testament. Love God with all your heart and soul and mind and strength. And love your neighbor as yourself."

That is *it*? Yes. First, you must love the Lord your God with all your heart, soul, mind, and strength. There is a word for that. In the Bible, the word for loving God with all your heart and soul and mind and strength is *worship*. Worship is expressing my love to God, and it is living for God's pleasure. Any time you express your love to God, any time you live to please God, you are *worshiping*. The problem today is that we have taken this word *worship* and have so watered it down. We have churches that are not really teaching; they are just entertaining. We have so watered it down that today worship has become a synonym for *music*. In fact—worse than that—it has become a *genre* of music! "I really like the fast praise songs, but I especially like the slow worship songs"—as if worship had anything to do with tempo.

Now I am going to shock you: there is no such thing as Christian music. There are only Christian lyrics. If I were to put on a record up here—does anyone remember records?—and it had no words on it, how would you know if it were a Christian song or not? A spiritual song? A sacred song? You would not because there are no sacred tunes, just sacred lyrics. It is the lyrics that make it spiritual and sacred. The fact is, this Sunday, all around the world in a thousand different tones and styles and tones of music, Jesus Christ will be praised in worship. Your style and preference of music says a whole lot more about your background than your theology. It depends on where you were raised. If you were raised in Japan then you like a certain tonal scale; if you were raised in the Middle East you like another tonal scale. You know what? God likes all kinds of music. I do not, and you do not, but he does.

Have you figured out that God likes variety? Just look around. You are not "one in a million"; you are one in six billion! God loves variety. Did you know that when God made insects he made over sixty thousand kinds of beetles? You would have thought four or five hundred varieties would have been enough. Oh *no*. He had to make *sixty thousand* kinds of beetles! John, Paul, Ringo, George, and I don't know how many others! But I do know those. God says, "I want you to love me," and you can bring pleasure to God through the variety that he created. I do not think that God cares two bits about the style of worship, as long as it is done in spirit and in truth.

So what does that mean, "in spirit and in truth?" God is not talking about the Holy Spirit in this particular verse; he is talking about *your* spirit. He is saying that worship needs to be authentic, and it needs to be accurate. It needs to be devotional, and it needs to be doctrinal. It needs to be in spirit and in truth. If it is authentic and accurate—not lip service—then God says, "I do not care what style it is, because I created you all to be different."

The number one thing you are going to do when you get to heaven is worship. So what does God want you to do while you are here on earth? What on earth are you here for? *Practice.* God wants you to learn to love him; he wants you to learn to know him. You can summarize the art of worship in one simple word: *offer.* "Offer your bodies as living sacrifices, holy and pleasing to God—this is your spiritual act of worship" (Rom. 12:1b, NIV). Offer.

Formed for His Family: Fellowship

Not only are we to love God, but the Bible also tells us to love our neighbors as ourselves. What is that all about? The Christian life is not just a matter of believing, it is a matter of belonging. Believing, belonging, and becoming. Many people go around saying, "I'm a believer!" Well, you could just as easily go around saying, "I'm a belonger," because when you step across that line and are born again, what are you born into? You are born into his family. The Bible says that not only were you planned for his pleasure, but also you were formed for his family. In Ephesians we read that God's unchanging plan has always been "to adopt us into his own family by bringing us to himself through Christ Jesus. This is what he wanted to do, and it gave him great pleasure" (Eph. 1:5, NLT). God wanted a family, and he wanted you to be a part of it. That is hard for me to believe, hard for me to comprehend. The Creator of the universe created me so I could become a part of his family. Now, your spiritual family will far outlast your physical family, because it is eternal. In Hebrews we read that Jesus and the people he makes holy all belong to the same family and that is why he "is not ashamed to call them his brothers and sisters" (Heb. 2:11, NLT).

Now the Bible teaches not only do we belong to Christ, but we also—and this is pretty radical—belong to each other. The Bible teaches over and over and over that if you are a believer you belong to other believers. I belong to you, you belong to me; we are in the same family. By the way, if you do not like fellowship, then you are not going to like heaven because fellowship is all that is going to happen up there!

God wants us not only to learn to love him but also to learn to love each other. Why? Because *God is love*! So he wants us to learn not only to worship but also to fellowship, and to learn to love each other because it is all about love. The Bible tells us that we are to love each other. You know, a lot of people know what John 3:16 says, but they do not know what 1 John 3:16 says. Do you? *"We understand what love is when we realize what Christ has done for us—he gave his life for us! That means we ought to give our lives to the brothers."* That is fellowship. Fellowship, like worship, is a word that has been so downgraded, so destroyed, and so watered down. Today, "fellowship" means coffee, cookies, and casual conversation in the most utilitarian building of the church, sitting on hard chairs with a really boring background. Let me tell you what fellowship *really* is. *Koinonia,* the Greek word we translate as fellowship, involves commitment to each other as we are to Jesus Christ. That is fellowship. Coming to that understanding of fellowship is a part of growth, of becoming more like Christ. It involves not only loving God with all your heart but also loving your neighbors, others in God's family. The Bible says we belong to each other and we need each other, and this relationship is called fellowship. There is an old bit of doggerel that captures the common failing:

> To dwell above with those we love, that will be a glory.
> To dwell below with those we know, that's another story.

But God wants us to learn to love not only in the ideal but in the real. You know how God teaches you real love? It is simple. He puts you around some unlovely people. In every church, in every small group, in every committee there are people whom I call EGRs: "Extra Grace Required." They just do not get all the social cues. Maybe they talk a little too much, or they are insecure so they dominate the conversation. They just do not accurately understand what is going on and tend to put people ill at ease. Every one of you know what I am talking about. In fact, if you do *not* know what I am talking about, then I hate to tell you this, but *it is you.* When I started talking about it, everyone knew whom I was talking about. But God says, "We need you! And you need us." It is easy to love people who are cool or lovely. If God is going to teach you real love, then he is going to put you around unlovely people, what I call heavenly sandpaper. He is going to rub you the wrong way.

I do not know why, but in America we have these "floating believers." They float from church to church to church to church. I want to tell you something: you cannot grow spiritually without the body of Christ. You cannot grow spiritually without fellowship. This is the difference between Christianity and all the other religions. In other religions, the holy people are the ones who go up on a mountain and isolate themselves from humanity so that they will be pure. God, however, says, "No! That's not the holy person! The holy person is Jesus, in the middle of the crowd with the prostitutes, and the lepers, and today he would be with people who have AIDS." Why? Because it is all about love, and you cannot learn to love in an ivory tower. You have to be with people, and you have to get with them.

I was coming up here to Oxford on a train, and there was a little part of the ticket that said "not good if detached." The same is true of believers. Let us say you are the hand in the body of Christ and you get lopped off this week. Next week you go over to this church, and the next week over to *that* church. You know what you are going to do? You will shrivel up and die. Disconnected from the church, Christians will shrivel up and die. The Bible calls a Christian without a church family an orphan. In fact, there are fifty-six commandments in the New Testament that you cannot obey unless you are a part of an active local church. Why? Because it is all about learning love. The more mature you become as a Christian, the more you will love the church. Jesus died for the church. Christ died for the church: that is how much he loves it. In Christ's family, we have family responsibilities. Love one another, care for one another, encourage one another, pray for one another, help one another, serve one another. A lady said to me once, "Oh, I'm a member of the invisible church." I said, "Really? That's wonderful. When you are sick and in the hospital, who visits you? The invisible pastor? Where do you give your invisible tithes? Where do you do your invisible 'one-anothers' that Christ commands you to do?" You have to be in community. We are better together. We were planned for God's pleasure and formed for his family. That is worship and family.

Created to Become Like Christ: Discipleship

The third purpose of life is this: the Bible says that you were created to become like Christ. In Romans we read, "For whom he did foreknow, he also did predestinate to be conformed to the image of his Son, that he might be the first-born among many brethren" (Rom. 8:29, KJV). God's goal for you is to grow up. What does the grown-up look like? Jesus. He is the model of maturity. I love *The Message* translation of Colossians 1:15: "We look at this Son and see God's original purpose in everything created." This is not God's "Plan B." It has been God's plan from the very beginning. When God created man, he said, "let us make man in our image." From the very beginning of time, it has been God's plan to make us in his image. Now do not misunderstand me. You are not ever going to be a God. He is talking about becoming godly. There are cults that teach that you become a god. No, God is saying that you become like him in character, in morals, in attitudes: like Christ. Let me just give you a little stress reliever (this has been really helpful to me): God is God, and you are not. I have found that so helpful. Every time I start pretending that I am God, there is a warning siren. Do you know what it is called? *Worry.* Worry is assuming that I am God, that I have to control it, that I am the general manager of the universe. Stress is the warning light that I am trying to be God! You are not God. I know there is all this new-age stuff that says, "you are the divine," but if you are God, why do you not solve all the problems in the world? You cannot even solve your own problems, much less those of the world! You are not a god, but the Bible says that you can become godly.

God is far more interested in what you are than what you do. Why? Because you are not taking your career to heaven, but you are taking your character. The Bible says we were created to become like Christ, and we are in an ever-maturing process. One day we shall see him and we shall become as he is; the firstborn among many brothers. I love 2 Corinthians 3:18, "And the Lord—who is the Spirit—makes us more and more like him." (NLT). You know, "from glory unto glory"; from one degree of maturity to another. The question then becomes: How does God do that? How does God make me like Jesus? If that is the third purpose of life, then how does he do it?

First, what is Jesus like? I think one of the best expressions of Jesus is the fruit of the Spirit: those nine qualities of love, joy, peace, patience, kindness, goodness, faithfulness, gentleness, and self-control that we find in Galatians 5. If you want a picture of Jesus, that is a good one. So how does God produce the fruit of the Spirit in my life? Am I just walking down the street one day and *zap!* I am filled with love and from that time onward I love everybody? I do not think so. Or one day I am just walking down the street and *zap!* I am suddenly filled with joy and the rest of my life is one solid piece of joy? No. The way God produces the fruit of the Spirit in your life is by allowing you to be in the exact opposite situation. You see, temptation is not always a temptation to be bad; it is also an opportunity to do good. Temptation is just a choice. You can look at it as a temptation to do bad or as a choice to do good. Every time you choose to do good you grow in character, as the Holy Spirit empowers you to make those decisions.

So how does God teach you love? We have already said that he will put you around unlovely people. How does God teach you joy? Well, joy is different from happiness. Happiness depends on happenings, on happenstances. It is circumstance-based. I go to Disney Land, and I am happy; I come out and realize how much money I have spent, and I am not happy. It is temporal. So how does God teach you real joy? In the middle of grief—in the world you will have tribulation. How about peace? By making everything go your way? Of course not! He teaches you peace in the middle of chaos. How does he teach us patience? Well, in America it is called the Department of Motor Vehicles. Standing in line, waiting in traffic jams, doctors offices.

Have you ever been in a hurry, and God was not? God's waiting rooms are some of the most difficult areas of life to handle. God is teaching you patience.

Here is the deal: if God is going to make us more like Jesus, then he is going to take us through everything Jesus went through! Were there times when Jesus was lonely? Yes. Tired? Yes. Tempted? Yes. Were there times when he was tempted to be discouraged? Yes. When he was misjudged and criticized? Yes. If God did not spare his own son from these things—and the Bible says in Hebrews that Jesus learned obedience through suffering, made perfect and mature through suffering—do you think that God would exempt you from the things he did not exempt his own Son from? Of course not! This is not heaven! This is earth! So many people misjudge, thinking that abundant life means fun and possessions and popularity. That is not the abundant life! This is earth, not heaven; this is the "get ready" stage. It is in heaven that there are no problems, no tears, no sorrows; all joy. That is why we are to pray: "Thy will be done on earth as it is in heaven!" In heaven, God's will is done *perfectly*, and on earth, it is not.

I was speaking recently at the Aspen Ideas Institute, and they were asking some very tough questions. I was actually asked to come and speak on the reality of evil in the world, and that was the day that the bombs went off in London. I wanted to say, "Uh—do I need to say *more*? Pick up the newspaper. Evil is a reality, and people can choose to do evil. And they do. But God is not the author of evil." God has a purpose, however, in every problem; and if God is going to make us like Christ, then he is going to take us through the things Christ went through. You can learn from any situation if you have the right attitude. We become like Christ, as Ephesians 4:13 says: "*we will become completely like him*" (CEV).

Shaped to Serve God: Ministry

Now there is a fourth purpose in life. The Bible says that we are shaped to serve God. We are going to serve God in eternity, so what does God want us to do here? Practice, so you know how to serve God. It is impossible to serve God directly here on earth. You cannot even see him. The only way to serve God on earth is by serving others. We are shaped to serve God. Job says, "your hands shaped me and formed me," (Job 10:8, NIV), and David says in Psalm 139:13 that he was created in his mother's womb. The Bible tells us in Ephesians 2:10 that God has made us what we are; he has created us to do good works in Christ Jesus, which he planned in advance for us to do. Before you were born, God wired you up to serve him in a certain way.

There is another name for this kind of service: ministry. Every Christian is a minister. Not every believer is a *pastor*, but if you are a believer then you are a minister. You are called, commissioned, and commanded to ministry because it just means service. The word *servant* and the word *minister* are the same word in the Greek: *diakonos*. I do not know why we have so much division over this because we are *all* called to serve. My wife likes to say that when you come to Christ he asks you to put on an apron and get ready to serve. A nonserving, nonministering Christian is a contradiction. The Bible says that God has uniquely shaped you to serve him. Of course, in Saddleback I love to make little acrostics, so I made one for this. I call it SHAPE—five ways you are wired to serve God:

> **S**piritual gifts
>
> **H**eart
>
> **A**bilities
>
> **P**ersonality
>
> **E**xperiences

These are the things that make you, you!

First, God gives you spiritual gifts. When you come to Christ he gifts you to do things for him. There are a lot of books on spiritual gifts, so the only problem is that I do not agree with them because they tend to make these regimented lists as if you can check off your spiritual gifts. We are *all unique*, and your gift of faith might be different from mine and from others. You cannot standardize spiritual gifts. I remember when I was a teenager I took a spiritual gifts test. I had not done any service, and I found out that the only gift I had according to that test was martyrdom. I said, "Oh great, that is the gift you get to use one time and it is *over*. And you only get to use it on the last day of your life!" I would never have known that I had the gift of teaching because I had never done it. It was not until I started doing it that people began to say, "You know, Rick, when you talk God blesses it." A lot of books these days tell you to discover your gift so that you will know your ministry. I believe the exact opposite. Just get involved in ministry, and you will discover what you are good at. You know, I actually started out in music ministry, because I have a heart to sing. The only problem is that no one wants to hear it. I made a joyful noise, but even pigs do that when they are rooting for acorns! So we all have spiritual gifts, things we are gifted to do.

We also have a heart, things we *love* to do. There are some things that turn you on, and some things bore you to tears. That is your heart. Did you know that not only do you have a unique physical thumbprint, footprint, voiceprint, "heartprint," but you have a unique *emotional* heartprint. That means that there are some things that you just love to do. Where do you think you got those natural interests and hobbies? God wired you that way; he gave you a heart, and he gave us all different hearts. Why? Because if everybody liked to do the same thing, a lot would be left undone. God wired us all, and some people love certain things and some people love others things. What you need to be aware of in Christian life today is what I call, not just "gift-projection," but "heart-projection": "You must care about everything that I care about with equal intensity!" Well, that is just not true, because we are all called to care about different things so that everything in the world gets done.

We also have abilities. Some of you are good at math, some at music, some at mechanics. Natural abilities you are given at birth, but spiritual gifts you are given at your second birth.

Some people so emphasize spiritual gifts that they ignore natural abilities. Where do you think they came from? They came from God! Your natural abilities are just as spiritual as your spiritual gifts. In the Bible there is no gift of computer programming, but do we need computer programmers in the body of Christ? Sure we do! The Bible does not even list music as a gift! It is a talent. If you have the gift of music, you got it when you were born, not when you were born again. But it is still just as spiritual.

You also have a personality. And do we have them all here today! Some of you like routine; some of you like variety. Some of you like working on a team; some of you are "lone rangers." Some of you like the theoretical; some of you like the concrete. Some of you are morning people; some of you are night people. Have you noticed that morning larks often marry night owls? It is God's sense of humor. He likes to put opposites together to watch the sparks fly. "This will be fun—watch this, it will be really cool!" When two people agree on everything, one of them is not necessary. When you eat, you eat with a knife and a fork; you do not use two forks.

Experiences are the things God uses to shape you to serve him. There are family experiences—and let me tell you something: there are accidental parents, but there are no accidental children. There are illegitimate parents, but no illegitimate children. God takes into account even our mistakes and our sins. Your parents may have been good, bad, or indifferent; they may have abandoned you! They may have been terrible parents, but really it is irrelevant because God was more interested in creating you than he was in their parenting skills. God knew that they had just the right DNA to create you. You are not an accident. You were made by God, and you were made for God, and until you understand that reality, life is not going to make sense.

You were planned for his pleasure, formed for his family, created to become more like Christ, and shaped to serve him. And he uses those experiences of life: family experiences, educational experiences, vocational experiences, all different kinds of experiences. Most important of all, God uses painful experiences. They are the number one way God shapes you to serve him. The thing that you regret the most, that you wish had never happened, that you try to hide the most, that you are most embarrassed about is the very thing that God wants to make your greatest ministry. God never wastes a hurt. We do, but he does not. God specializes in bringing good out of bad. Anybody can bring good from good; that is no big deal. God turns crucifixions into resurrections. He turns bad into good. Who can better help parents of a Down's syndrome child than the parents of a Down's syndrome child? Who can better help somebody going through the pain of a divorce than someone who went through the pain of a divorce? Who can better help somebody struggling with an addiction to alcohol or drugs than someone who struggled with an addiction to alcohol or drugs? Who can better help someone who was raped or molested than someone who was raped or molested? The very thing that brings the most pain in your life, God wants to use, if only you will be honest with him, with yourself, and with others. You see, when you operate out of your strengths, people say, "So what? You're good at it, I'm not." But when you operate out of your weakness, people say, "Well, if God could use her, maybe God could use me!" That is why Paul says, "I glory in my weakness!"

I was born with a brain malfunction. They thought it was epilepsy, but it was not epilepsy. I grew up taking all kinds of medications because I would faint all the time. Even today, when adrenaline hits my system something like blindness—not blindness, but like a cheesecloth—hits me. When I stand up to speak and adrenaline hits my system, I cannot see until that adrenaline drains out. It is a very rare disorder; I have been to all the top clinics in the world, and they said they may name a syndrome after me! There are only fourteen or fifteen people they know of who have it. It makes public speaking excruciatingly painful. Everyone knows that adrenaline is a public speaker's best friend: if you do not have adrenaline, you are *boring*. You need it for passion. So when I get up to speak, adrenaline hits my system like any public speaker. I am not talking about nerves; I speak to 22,000 people every Sunday morning. I am not talking about stage fright. I have spoken in the Superdome three times. I have spoken to over a million people at one time. But when adrenaline hits my system, I go almost blind until it drains out. When I got up here, you did not know it; but I could not see you. I could not even see my notes.

When I started Saddleback Church, I said, "Well, I could do one service, but I could never do two." It was twenty-five years ago—I was twenty-five years old and had just moved there. I had no money, no members, no friends. I had just finished my master's degree and my doctorate and had just moved to California. With seven members we started on a January afternoon in 1980. Now, I am a country boy. I was raised in a village of less than 500 people, and I pulled into the L.A. area where God had told me to plant a church where I had no money, members, buildings, or acquaintances. I did not know a single person in the area. We got there in the middle of rush hour traffic, and I looked at all the cars and said, "God, you've got the wrong guy! What am I doing here?" We pulled off the interstate and walked into a real-estate office. I met a man named Don Dale on January 1, 1980. I said to him, "My name is Rick Warren. I'm twenty-five years old, and I'm here to start a church. I don't have any money, I don't have any buildings, I don't have any members, and I need a place to live." He just laughed and said, "Let's see what we can do." Well, where God guides, God provides. Within two hours he found us a little apartment, and we signed the papers on it. He got us the first month rent-free, no money down, and that man became the first member of my church. I had said to him, "Don, do you go to church anywhere? No? Hey—you're the first member of my church!"

So we started with seven people. I preached the first sermon. My wife did not like it, and it has been downhill ever since. On Easter this year we celebrated our twenty-fifth anniversary, and I, the guy who hates to do public speaking, did *thirteen services* for the 45,400 who showed up. On that day, 4460 people gave their lives to Christ. I walked backstage and thought: "In my weakness you are strong." Of all the people God could have chosen, he chose a guy who hates public speaking. Some people like being in front of a crowd, being a ham; I do not. I would not do it. Do you know why I do it? Because I am addicted to changing lives! I do not like preaching, but I love the results of it. I love watching the Holy Spirit transform individuals before my very eyes. So whatever your weakness is, God can use it for good; and your greatest ministry can actually come out of it!

Made for a Mission: Evangelism

There is a fifth purpose: you were made for a mission. God wants you to tell others about him. Jesus said in John 17:18, "In the same way that you gave me a mission in the world, I give them a mission in the world" (*The Message*). Here is the difference between ministry and mission: every believer needs a ministry in the church and a mission in the world. They are not the same. Ministry is for believers; missions are for unbelievers. Jesus said, "I'm giving you a mission in the world." You need a ministry that edifies the family of God, and a mission that is reaching out to others. God wants you to have both in your life. The Bible tells us that we have been given the ministry of reconciliation, bringing people back to Christ. Last week I had the most amazing privilege. The president of Rwanda wrote me a note about a year ago and told me that he had read *The Purpose Driven Life*, and that he was now a man of purpose. The book had changed his life. He said, "We want Rwanda to be the first purpose-driven nation!" So he invited me to come and do the Global Peace Plan, which I wish I had time to tell you about: planting churches, equipping leaders, caring for the poor and the sick, and educating the next generation. I have seen 4500 of my members go overseas in the last two years in forty-seven countries quietly testing a thing called the "Peace Plan," which we are going to release and which I hope will make a difference in our world.

Last week I spent three days training the church leaders of Rwanda, and meeting with the business leaders of Rwanda, and the cabinet of Rwanda. We met with the government, and I met with the Parliament. On the last day, we had a national reconciliation rally between the Hutus and the Tutsis, eleven years after the genocide. The president spoke and invited me to be the main speaker that day. He set it up, and I got up and talked about the ministry of reconciliation in a nation where a million people were killed in a genocide and now are living next to each other. This is not like Israel, where there is a fence between the Palestinians and the Jews. In Rwanda, the people who hacked up your family are living right next to you, and there is no division. We held a rally, and I asked for two testimonies: the testimony of a perpetrator and the testimony of a victim, both of whom had found forgiveness in Christ, forgiven each other, and had become friends. They shared their testimonies. Then I spoke on reconciliation and said, "You know, the Bible says that in Christ there is neither slave nor free, Jew nor Gentile, male or female, nor Hutu or Tutsi. You are Rwandans, and you are one in Christ!" The place exploded in applause, laughter, and praise. It was an amazing sight in the national stadium, and only God can do that.

Fulfilling your mission in the world is called evangelism. There are a lot of people who will say, "Oh, I don't like this church growth stuff. It's all ego." Most of the world, even most of the church, just does not realize how much lost people matter to God. They just do not get it. They do not get it that the Bible says that God is "not willing that any should perish but that all should come to repentance"(2 Pet. 3:9, NKJV). As long as there is one person within driving distance of your church that does not know Christ, you are commanded to reach out. It is not an option. We do not grow for our benefit; we grow because there are people without Christ going to a Christ-less eternity. We grow because there are people without Jesus who need the Lord, and because everybody needs Jesus. The church that does not want to grow is saying to the world, "you can go to hell." That is just being honest. It takes unselfish people to grow a church. It is very easy to say, "Oh, we're all saved. Us four, no more!" It is easy to have our quaint little groups, but we do not really care about getting our hands dirty, reaching out, or starting additional services. At Saddleback Church, we have six service times on Sunday and twenty-two different services. Why? Because we have to hold all those people. It is hard work, folks. Why do we do that? For ego? Of course not! We do it because Jesus shed his blood for those people and he wants everybody to know him! Saddleback now has 82,000 names on its role, and people now say, "How big should a church get?" That is the wrong question. We should be saying, "Should anyone be left behind? Does anyone deserve to be left behind?" We care because God cares.

My dad was a man on a mission. He pastored for about fifty years, and he never pastored a church of more than about one hundred people. But he was a great carpenter, and he took lay teams all around the world. In his lifetime, my dad built over 150 church buildings—small church buildings all around the world on nearly every continent. He died a couple years ago, and in his last days (he was dying of cancer, and it had spread and hit his brain) he began to be delusional. He dreamed aloud for an entire week. It was an amazing experience. I sat there in that room with my dad for the last week of his life listening to him dream aloud. You know, you can learn a lot about a person by listening to his dreams. In that week, I never once heard my dad talk about any books he had read, movies he had gone to, fishing trips (and he dearly loved fishing), being a World War II hero (which he was); what I heard him talk about almost twenty-four hours a day for the last week of his life was building churches. He would say, "Now make sure that team gets back for the meal! Get the lumber over there. When the joists fit together, make sure the electricity is off." He just relived building all these churches. Two nights before he died, I knew I was going to have to leave the next day to go speak at Max Lucado's church. I did not want to leave. As I was sitting in that room, however, with my wife and my niece, Alyssa, my dad became very agitated and tried to get out of bed. My wife,

Kay, said, "Jimmy, you've got to lie down." But he kept trying to get out of bed. She said, "Jimmy, you're dying! You have to lie down! You have to lay still." But he just kept trying to get out of bed. Finally, my wife said, "Jimmy, *what do you want?*" And my dad said, "Gotta save one more for Jesus! Gotta save one more for Jesus!" He began to say that over and over and over. I am not making this up or exaggerating: he said it maybe 150 times in the next hour. I bowed my head sitting next to the bed, tears rolling down my face, and thanked God for a father like that. That was what was on his heart in the last days of his life. He reached up his hand—his very frail hand—and in front of my wife and my niece he put his hand on my head, as if in blessing, and said, "Save one more for Jesus!"

I intend for that to be the theme for the rest of my life, because there is nothing more important than that. If you know something more important to do with your life than to help people find out that they are not an accident, that they were made to last forever, that God made them to love them, that Christ died for them; to help introduce them to Christ, help them grow to maturity in Christ, and help them find a church home and get involved in a family and fellowship; to help them to discover their giftedness and to serve other people, going out into the world to bring others to Christ, all to the glory of God—if you know something more important than that, then I invite you to stand up right now and tell us all, because I decided a long time ago that I am not going to waste my life. And I have not.

In the next 365 days in my state of California, 231,000 people will die, and most of them will go into an eternity without Jesus Christ. In the next 365 days in my country of America, 2.3 million Americans will die, and most of them will go into eternity without Jesus Christ. In the next 365 days, 54 million people in this world will die, and most of them will go into eternity without Jesus Christ. As we think about the good and the true and the beautiful, and what the purpose of it all is, just remember that the purpose is to bring glory to God. And how do we bring glory to God? By doing what he put us on this earth to do. He made us to love us, and wants us to know and love him back: that is worship. He made us to learn to love each other because he is love and he wants us to be like him: that is fellowship. He made us to grow in Christ's likeness: that is discipleship. We are to be conformed to the image of Christ! He made us to serve God by serving others. We practice these things because we are ready for eternity. As C. S. Lewis said, we are not made for time, but for eternity.[2] That is the message we must share in every sphere of life—in the political, the social, the academic, the entertainment world; every area of life! Sports, church, business!

I am praying for a new reformation. We had a reformation 500 years ago, but it was a reformation of belief. We do not need a reformation of belief—we know what we believe—we need a reformation of behavior. The problem is that we are not doing what we know we believe. The first reformation was one of creeds; we need one of deeds. We need not a reformation but a mobilization, where the church becomes the church in the world. The Bible says that the church is the body of Christ, but today the hands and the feet have been amputated, and all that is left is a mouth. We do a lot of talking, and not a whole lot else. Most of the time we are known for what we are against instead of what we are for. I am praying that we will reattach the hands and feet to the body of Christ and be the hands and feet to the world for Jesus and for his glory.

---

[2]C. S. Lewis, *The Screwtape Letters* (New York: HarperSanFrancisco, 2001), 75.

An Allegory

Desire knows what she wants,
    and when she wants it.
Demands come easily for one
    who easily makes up her mind.
Never satisfied but quickly mollified,
    like a rapacious shark,
    her frenzy subsides when appeased,
    only to rise again with more demands
    for more of the same.
Any one of many will do,
    for Desire feeds on the experience,
    not the food.

Longing casts an indifferent eye
    at every enticement.
Desperately she searches
    for she knows not what.
Never at peace, she prowls
    with feline disdain
    over the overtures and offers
    that would divert her
    from her quest.
Only one thing will do,
    for Longing thirsts
    and cannot be quenched by dust.

Jackson, Tenn.
Summer 2004

5

The Good, the True, and the Beautiful in the Psalmist's Pursuit of God

David Dockery

TEXT: Psalm 84

It has been said that getting to know God is like falling in love. For some, it is head-over-heels love at first sight, with a rush to the altar. But others are reluctant converts, such as the one for whom this conference is named, who find the whole idea of pursuing the knowledge of God wholly to their unliking, only to discover along the way that many of their first impressions were mistaken. A begrudging acceptance moves toward appreciation and then, almost unnoticed, slips over the line into heartfelt embrace. Yet, in either case Malcolm Muggeridge was right in observing that in the end, like the psalmist in Psalm 84, he found that getting to know God was like "a homecoming, of picking up the threads of a lost life, of responding to a bell that had long been ringing, of taking a place at a table that had long been vacant."[1]

---

[1]Malcolm Muggeridge, *Confessions of a 20th-Century Pilgrim* (San Francisco: Harper & Row, 1988), 13, quoted online at http://www.thewords.com/articles/mugquest.htm.

But then for some of us romance crashes into reality. We give ourselves to God, and then we struggle profoundly with the relationship. We are drawn in, and then find ourselves wanting to flee in fear. We move from trust to confusion, from faith to fear, from intimacy to doubt. We find that living with God is not easy.

Many of us respond to the struggle with a self-imposed guilt, presuming that faith should somehow be free of complexity and challenge. We blame ourselves, responding to the struggle with resentment and placing "God in the dock."

The 84th Psalm is a picture of one who longs for God and the good things of God. The psalmist, who probably also wrote a similar hymn in Psalm 42, is not writing about some shallow escape from his current challenges. No, here is a picture of one who longed to meet God—to genuinely know God. The psalmist acknowledges that such an experience is a pilgrimage, a long journey that has obstacles and difficulties along the way. But, as the psalmist discovered, even while we are going through the Valley of Baca (v. 6), the valley of tears, God remains good and true.

Like the psalmist, most of us can point to a place, a time, a situation, in which God was especially real to us. In a few months, I will guess that some of you may point back to this place, to this week, as a time like that. For Abraham it was Bethel; for Moses, it was Mt. Sinai; for the psalmist it was the dwelling place of God which he describes as "lovely," as a place of beauty, which was most likely the temple of Solomon.

The psalmist, however, was away from that beautiful place—he may have been in exile or in prison, he may have been ill, or off to battle; however, for some reason of which we cannot be sure, he could not get back to that place where he longed to meet God.

It is difficult to understand the impression that the temple made on the Hebrew worshiper. David proposed the temple and amassed the materials, but Solomon coordinated its construction. One commentator has said it was made of one hundred thousand talents of gold and a million talents of silver, a multi-billion dollar project—because of the value of precious metals by today's standards. It took seven and a half years to complete. Thirty thousand Israelites and a hundred fifty thousand Canaanites were recruited as hewers of stone, carriers of water, and builders of the temple. The beauty was impressive, but God's presence was overwhelming—for it was here they met the living God (v. 2—one of only two places that God is called the living God in the Psalms). It was here that the true and living God was worshiped and adored as the source of all that is beautiful and good and true.

We today, individually and collectively according to 1 Corinthians 3 and 1 Corinthians 6, are the temple of God. In the Old Testament, God had a temple for his people; in the New Testament, He has a people for His temple.

The kind of longing for God described in Psalm 84 should then characterize us this morning. While the psalmist longed for the House of God, he ultimately longed for God Himself. Likewise for us as well, while we long for the good, the true, and the beautiful, we ultimately long for the true, and we long for the living God as Professors McGrath and Kreeft described so well yesterday, the one who is the Creator of all that is beautiful, the source of all that is true, and the wellspring of all that is good. Three times the psalmist proclaims that happy and blessed are those whose heart, whose strength, whose life is focused on God. Perhaps James 4:8 captures the first part of this Psalm—"Come near to God and he will come near to you" (NIV). But the process of following God, like the actual pilgrimage of the Israelites to Jerusalem, can be a fatiguing and trying experience. Along the journey, we will likely pass through the Valley of Baca (v. 6), which can manifest itself in many ways. It may be an illness, a time of severe temptation, a season of grief, a period of reversal in our work, an emotional trauma in our family. Yet the pilgrimage with God will likely include crossing this valley—creating times of great reflection, as with C. S. Lewis in *The Problem of Pain*. Like the biblical writers themselves, our experience is filled with questions.

Usually our response is the often-asked question of *why*? Some of you, especially those from the United States, may occasionally still watch the old *Andy Griffith* reruns. There is one episode where Barney is showing the Mayberry kids, Opie and his friends, around the sheriff's office. On the bulletin board are the most wanted pictures. One of the boys, intrigued by the pictures, asked Barney if these were real photographs of the wanted people. Barney proclaims, "Yes, and they are vicious criminals," to which the boy responds, "Well, why didn't they just keep them here when they took these pictures?" "*Why?*"—an often-asked question.

Do you ever wonder "why?"? You tell people that there are 400 billion stars in the sky, and they say they believe you. Tell those same people a park bench has wet paint, and they want to touch it. Why is that?

Why are there five syllables in the word *monosyllabic*? Why doesn't glue stick to the inside of a bottle? But more significantly, "Why?" is the question that comes to our lips when life-stopping events happen as we cross the Valley of Baca. Yet the psalmist says an amazing thing happens there. You can dig down through the arid valley floor and find springs. The impossible becomes possible, affliction can be turned into joy, ashes to beauty, hardship to rejoicing, and—as verse seven suggests—weakness can be turned to strength.

At this very moment more people in this room than we might think are probably walking through difficult and dry places on their journeys with God. Difficulties such as illness, depression, despair, losses, trials, and tests have dried out our lives. But like the psalmist, our lives can become an oasis. Longing for God generates renewed resources. As Paul writes in 2 Corinthians 3:18, we "are being transformed into his likeness with ever-increasing glory" (NIV).

The psalm concludes with the "Hope of Renewal." Those who desire to know God (vv. 1–4) and who set out on the journey to seek God (vv. 5–8) will experience renewal with God—for with God all things will become new.

Now the psalmist is at a place in his life ready to meet God, to celebrate His goodness, to adore His beauty, and to know

His truth. The encounter with God leads him to sing, "Better is one day in your courts / than a thousand elsewhere" (v. 10a, NIV)—don't you love that?

Our writer then goes on to say that he prefers the lowest place with God to the highest place without God. What an amazing statement! He can make it because he recognized that God is the only one who fulfills our ultimate longings.

When the questions spring up in our lives while we are going through the Valley of Baca, God sometimes seems distant. When that happens, what should we do? Assume He is not there? Assume He is there, but He doesn't care? Assume He is there, but He is unable to help?

No, I don't think so. Psalm 84 points us in totally different directions. Today, let us join the psalmist's longing for the beauty of God's dwelling place; let us trust the goodness of God; let us believe the truth of his Word. The ending verses form a promise for us:

For the Lord God is a sun and shield;
      he bestows favor and honor.
No good thing does the Lord withhold
      from those who walk uprightly.
O Lord of hosts,
      happy is everyone who trusts in you.
                              (vv. 11–12, NRSV)

Let us pray together.

Almighty and everlasting God, whom saints and angels delight to worship, we praise you for your word—even as we thank you for your presence with us today. We pray that you will enable us by your truth, we ask that you fill us with your goodness, and we pray that you will grant to us even now glimpses of your beauty—for our souls long for you, O Lord. We too want to say, "Better is one day in your courts than a thousand elsewhere." Help us to learn to serve you, the one true and living God, with joy and gladness for the sake of your Son and our Savior, Jesus the Christ, to whom be glory both now and forever. Amen.

Edisto Woodlands

My father took me in a wood to walk the forest floor,
And see the girth of trees such as I'd never seen before.
Beside the Edisto the forest stood in sanctity,
Reflecting in its ancient boughs with awesome majesty
The timeless depths from which it grew, from which it
    had its birth,
The depths that proffered life to man, and proffered life
    to earth.
Forgotten pagans deified the sylvan solitude,
And worshipped oak and terebinth with fervent attitude.
Perceiving in the groves of trees a presence and a force,
They deified the garden, thinking they had found the
    source
Of life, and health, and happiness, and all serenity,
For in its paths they felt the presence of eternity.
The trees of Canaan now are dust, the trees of Britain ash;
The forest on the Edisto, a scandal to abash
The race that spoiled the woodland, stands no more for
    eyes to see.
No child shall ever plumb its depths to marvel at a tree.
Once banished from the garden by the gardener's decree,
The offspring of the world now lack his sensitivity.
The trees were never sacred, nor professed to deity,
But through their shadows wandered in a soft solemnity
The lonely gardener we ignored while gazing at the trees,
In every other place on Earth, forgotten by degrees.
Yet in the wooded spots that we have blithely left behind,
The gardener's song can still be heard within the quiet
    mind.

Louisville, Ky.
1986

6

Another Genesis

James Jones

Service of Evensong, Ely Cathedral

TEXT: Genesis 1:31

What a grand theme—"Making All Things New: The Good, the True, and the Beautiful."

Let me come straight to the point, or rather to the three points of this sermon based on your Summer Institute theme—The Good, the True, and the Beautiful. According to the scriptures these three are easily indisputable.

The Good is all that God has made: "God saw everything that he had made, and indeed, it was very good" (Gen. 1:31, NRSV). The Good is all God's creation. The True is the one who came from above into the world full of grace and truth. His name is Jesus, and he declared himself to be the Truth. Here was the truest human being ever to walk the face of the earth. The Beautiful are those who express by any means possible—by art, by music, by song, by poetry, by sculpture, by painting, by drama, by dance, by body, by voice, by hands, and even by feet. Yes, according to the prophet Isaiah, even by feet, the Beautiful are the feet of those who assume peace, who bring good news, who announce salvation, who proclaim, "Your God reigns" (Is. 52:7, NRSV).

I am almost inclined to say that's the end of the sermon. My wife would be delighted. Her only advice to me about preaching is, "Keep it short!" But, I fear you might feel rather shortchanged. Not least because—in spite of the three great motifs of your conference—the world feels oppressed by the bad, the false, and the ugly, which calls for some Christian apologia, some explanation as to how these two dynamics exist in the world and whether and how they might be resolved.

This was, of course, one of the great themes of C. S. Lewis in his own writing—the conflict between good and bad, truth and falsehood, beauty and ugliness, and he deals with these in the Chronicles of Narnia.

I know that Lewis urged caution on those who wanted to read the Narnia stories as an exact allegory, and, therefore, to see a parallel in every character and incident. But it's clear from the books themselves that Lewis intended Narnia to be a symbol of the world in which we live.

In *The Last Battle,* Lord Digory explained the meaning of Narnia:

> When Aslan said you could never go back to Narnia, he meant the Narnia you were thinking of. But that was not the real Narnia. That had a beginning and an end. It was only a shadow or copy of the real Narnia, which has always been here and always will be here…You need not mourn over Narnia, Lucy. All of the old Narnia that mattered, all the dear creatures, have been drawn into the real Narnia through the Door. And of course it is different; as different as a real thing is from a shadow…His voice stirred everyone like a trumpet as he spoke these words: but when he added under his breath, "It's

all in Plato, all in Plato: bless me, what *do* they teach them at these schools!" the older ones laughed.[1]

Narnia is just a "shadow of the real thing," just as Plato believed that the world was but a shadow of the real and eternal world.

Lewis quoted and approved of Plato's "Allegory of the Cave." You will remember that in Plato's allegory, human beings were chained in a cave and, unable to look behind themselves to see the source of light, saw only the shadows on the wall. They thought the shadows were the real thing, the real world. Plato used this allegory to suggest that all the world we inhabit is ephemeral.

I have always found the allegory to be strikingly prophetic. Written six hundred years before Christ, it goes on to imagine what would happen should someone appear unchained to tell the truth about the shadows and the light. Plato, with rare insight into human nature, leaves no doubt that instead of welcoming such a truth-teller with open arms, they would rather kill him. This is exactly what they did to Jesus, who knew human hearts and that we often prefer darkness to light.

But although I find Plato's allegory prophetic, I have to say that I have reservations about his understanding of reality and about his influence on Christian thinking about the Good, the True, and the Beautiful. Let me put it in a question. Is creation good in itself, or is it simply a shadow of something else that is good? This is a much more serious question than it first appears.

Many Christians today see creation as transient, ephemeral, and ultimately to be discarded. They may not be signed-up Platonists, but they subscribe to what I once heard described as "a theology of obliteration." The earth will be consumed by fire and destroyed; then God will establish his kingdom. It is not a million miles away from Plato's view that the material world was less than good and that the body, although beautiful, was

---

[1]C. S. Lewis, *The Last Battle* (New York: Collier, 1976), 169–70.

basically a prison for the spirit, the divine spark that longed to be released at death from the tyranny of the flesh. Such a view profoundly affects how you view the present world; it makes a difference to how you treat the earth; it shapes your attitude and your behavior at every level, from the personal to the political.

If the earth is not originally and essentially good, if the earth is but a shadow of the real thing, if the earth is destined to be consumed in destruction by fire, then there can be no moral barrier to milking the earth for all that it is worth while you have time. If you couple this view to the belief that humankind is the apex of all creation and that all that exists is for our pleasure, you can understand why many Christians remain unconvinced and unpersuaded by the growing concern for the environment.

Here, I declare my own position. I am not so sure that this is what the Bible teaches about the world we inherit. Creation is not just a shadow of the real thing. It is real in itself and good. Although deeply affected by evil and sin and marked by the wounds of battle, creation has not lost its original goodness. Furthermore, and most importantly, God has not abandoned his creation. It is his expressed will and desire "to make all things new"—not by destroying all that he had made, rubbing it out and starting all over again; but, rather, by transforming, restoring, and renewing all that he has made and continues to sustain.

I remember years ago after I preached on this theme, a lady approached me to say that it reminded her of her first drawing classes as an art student. She had been told—and had never forgotten—when you make a mistake that you must never use an eraser. Instead, always work with the line to redeem it. Neither is God in the business of rubbing out that which he has made. Such a theology has a profound effect on how we view and treat the earth. "The earth is the LORD's, and everything in it" (Ps. 24:1, NIV).

I know some Christians become rather agitated at this idea, fearing that a concern for the environment is a lapse into paganism and New Age. The reason such groups have made such headway, and especially among the young, is because Christians have vacated the ground so clearly staked out in scripture.

"The earth is the LORD's!" That's the basic premise for our concern for the future of the planet. Furthermore, Paul tells us in Colossians, "for in him all things in heaven and on earth were created…all things have been created through him and for him" (Col. 1:16, NRSV). Seldom has such a high christology been founded upon three such small words—in, through, and for. In the same passage Paul trumpets the great work of redemption and reconciliation that belongs uniquely to Christ, through whom "God was pleased to reconcile to himself all things, whether on earth or in heaven by making peace through the blood of his cross" (Col. 1:20, NRSV).

This is how God makes all things new. He entrusts the task to his son. In so doing he declares just how good his creation is—it is worth saving, it is worth redeeming, it is worth reconciling to himself. It is worth speaking the Truth. That is why those who announce this salvation, who proclaim the sovereignty of God over all creation, who give expression to this peace, this shalom, this wholeness are described by the prophet as beautiful, for they declare the beauty of God's holiness.

When earlier this month the leaders of the G8 Nations met in Scotland, the British Prime Minister who was in the chair put at the top of their agenda poverty in Africa and climate change. Various commentators offered different critiques—scientific, economic, and ethical. For example, the academies of science of the G8 countries pronounced that the scientific evidence for our carbon emissions affecting the climate was overwhelming; the economists agreed about the impact controlling their emissions would have on the economies of the G8; campaign groups lobbied hard on the moral imperatives of making poverty history, especially on the continent of Africa.

What was missing from all these valuable commentaries was a theological critique, and it is here in your conference theme. God is making all things new, and so must we, for how can we not go with what God is making? God is making all things new. He takes his creation, originally good but marred by evil and sin, and redeems it to make it perfectly good.

God is making all things new. The chosen agent of this redemption is none other than the agent of its creation—the one and only one who is True, Jesus Christ.

God is making all things new. That is the theological reason for caring about the earth and our environment. And all who move with God for the salvation of the earth and its beauty are in the eyes of God deemed "beautiful."

In the last of the Narnia stories, *The Last Battle*, Lewis describes the devastation of Narnia by the Dragons and Great Lizards. It is a passage of remarkable contemporary resonance:

> They went to and fro tearing up the trees by their roots and crunching them up as if they were sticks of rhubarb. Minute by minute the forests disappeared. The whole country became bare...The grass died. Soon Tirian found that he was looking at a world of bare rock and earth. You could hardly believe that anything had ever lived there.[2]

Two years ago I was in Central America and had the opportunity of flying over several of those countries. I saw with my own eyes what I had been told from maps—that over the last fifty years, Central America has lost eighty percent of its rain forests, with all the devastation that has brought to the environment and to the biodiversity of the region and the world. I took this flight over Honduras and Nicaragua in a small four-seater plane. Painted on the side of this missionary plane were these words: "Jesus is Lord." Lord, not of a shadow, but of the real thing. Lord not just of Heaven, but of Earth. Lord of the whole creation. In and for and through Jesus all this creation came into being. Jesus, Lord not of a shadow, but of the real thing. And he is making all things new. And so must we.

---

[2]Ibid., 155.

The forests are the lungs of the earth. Such raping of the earth is bad, ugly, and unsustainable, and contrary to God's providence. The devastation of the earth is a desecration of all that is good, true, and beautiful. It is ultimately a blasphemy, for it is to go against the purposes of God, which are to make all things new.

To allow the bad, the false, and the ugly is to resist our Lord's own prayer that we should pray for the doing of God's will on earth as it is done in heaven. God save us and the whole earth from the bad, the false, and the ugly. Let the good, the true, and the beautiful be our heart's desire as we work with God to make all things new.

Incarnation

"Come out! Come out,
wherever you are!"
Hiding in a burning bush!
Hiding in a stack of smoke!
Hiding in the wind and fire!
Never seems to be there
when you want him,
But always seems to be
looking over your shoulder.
But if he ever showed
his face around here,
We'd nail him
to the wall!

Nashville, Tenn.
April 8, 2004

Welcoming the Unwelcome

Richard Lloyd-Morgan

Text: Matthew 11:28

Why should we feel surprised by the joy of meeting new friends? Why should it be anything other than a journey of excitement and wonder when we are given the time and space to expand our circle of acquaintance? Is it, perhaps, that sometimes we try to bring our own agendas, our own little soap boxes, into the frame? Are we sometimes in danger of trying to shape a new friendship into what we would have it be before we have even got the measure of the person whom we have only just encountered? How sad and how limiting is that? How unimaginative is that? We have our own sets of values, to be sure; but how often do we find that God is speaking to us through the medium of another person, and we are deaf because we do not much care for, or are uncomfortable with, the language or the idiom that we are hearing? This condition applies to Christians just as much as to others. In fact, sometimes, one suspects rather more so.

To effect this journey of encountering new friends, of expanding our circle of acquaintance, we must be prepared to

71

leave home. Leaving home can be dangerous. Cocooned within our own safety zone—secure, if you like, behind the white picket fence of what we know and what we trust—we will face no threat of opposition or of challenge. But how limiting and fundamentally how dull our life will be if we restrict ourselves to what is always safe.

I heard recently a woman talking on the radio, complaining bitterly that sometimes at the end of sentences, but often enough so that she registered it, at the end of conversations with friends, as a parting shot the friend would say, "Well, goodbye now. Take care." She said she did not want to "take care." She wanted, above all, to take risks. I echo that. To realize the excitement and the challenge of the new, we have to leave the safety of our own burrows and journey Bilbo-like, Frodo-like, into new and uncharted lands. What I am saying is nothing new.

Many of you here today will have traveled huge distances, and for some that may well have been a challenge, and was, or is, even hard to accomplish for any number of reasons. For others it will have been easy. Travel broadens the mind, we are informed. So it may be, but the journey that broadens our knowledge and our understanding of other people is crucial to what we can call our humanity. Jesus himself was constantly journeying. He seemed to stay in one place for only short periods of times: "Foxes have holes and birds of the air have nests, but the Son of Man has no place to lay his head" (Lk. 9:58, NIV). And so it may have been, and although it may have been unsettling for him, and baffling to us who crave the comforts of a home and all the security that that home affords, it ensured that he was able to meet people where they were, both literally as well as figuratively.

There are very few occasions when we hear of Jesus turning anyone away. There were times, to be sure, when he suggested that there was work to be done before someone was in a position to realize his or her full potential, such as the rich young man who was advised to go home and sell everything that he possessed.

The overwhelming evidence that we have, however, is that Jesus' ministry was one of welcome, acceptance, and healing. He fed people. He restored people to fullness of life. He nourished people with the richness of his gospel, and though they may have been challenged, though they may have had to go home and rethink the whole approach to their lives, people were not turned away—and certainly never because they did not come up to scratch in terms of not being virtuous enough.

Jesus' ministry, and by extension our ministry (and it is by no means limited to men and women who wear a dog collar) is to "make all things new." In his book *The Four Loves,* C. S. Lewis quotes Ovid, who said that to be loved, we must first become lovable. Now this may be true in human terms, but it absolutely is not true in Gods terms. God's welcome is for all people, whatever their circumstances, whatever their personality. It is not for us to judge. "Come to me, all you who are weary and burdened, and I will give you rest" (Mt. 11:28, NIV), not, "I might refresh you provided that you have achieved a sufficiently high grade in your goodness studies." Jesus said, "Suffer the little children to come unto me, and forbid them not: for of such is the kingdom of God" (Mk. 10:14, KJV). We are all little children, struggling constantly to fulfill our true potential, to become the adult creatures that God created us to be. There are times when it is easier than at others, but God's welcome is not qualified, not conditional. His welcome is something for which we can only offer our heartfelt, grateful thanks.

Can I, by way of example, give you two small instances of unexpected welcome that have resonated with me recently? Last May I was staying with friends in Washington state, and I had the opportunity to meet Kim Gilnett in Seattle in order to talk through some issues that might arise at this conference. Now Kim did not know me from a bar of soap, but his welcome to me, a complete stranger, was immediate and warm. He gave me his time and a very, very good lunch down at Ivan's on the waterside. I felt, and it sounds incredibly cliché, but I felt valued and affirmed and all the things that go with the feeling of warmth and being surprised by joy to be in the presence of somebody who just seemed to be pleased to be in my presence.

Another time I was working in Scotland, in Glasgow, and I went one Sunday morning to the service of eucharist at St. Mary's Episcopal Cathedral. For some reason that now completely escapes me, I was in a vile, leprous mood. I have not wanted to go back too far in case I remember why I was in a vile and leprous mood, but I was. The last thing I wanted was to be any part of any worshiping community, but I thought, "I'd better go to church because that's what you do on a Sunday morning." So I aimed for the very back row of St. Mary's, and in good Anglican tradition, because I had got there rather late, all the back rows were already full. I had to go nearer the front. Squeezing myself past various people so that I could hug a pillar, and therefore be as out of sight and out of range as was humanly possible, I made myself as inconspicuous as I could so that I could say at the end of the service with complete justification that nobody had noticed me, nobody had welcomed me, nobody had made me feel at home. Well, come the peace and the sharing of the peace, the provost of the cathedral, who is a great and good man called Griff Dines, whom I had met once or possibly twice a year or two before, said, "Let us offer one another a sign of peace." I was standing there with hands thrust deep into my trouser pockets, and he came straight down the nave, leant right across the people who were sitting next to me with outstretched hand and said, "Peace be with you Richard. It's very good to have you with us in Glasgow again." I wanted to weep. Why? Only because one person's human gesture of welcome had completely turned my day upside down, on its head. Someone made me realize that I was visible and valuable. Griff, naturally, will not remember a thing about it, because people who do these things as a matter of course never do, but I have never forgotten it.

In King's Chapel we have been trying for some months to extend our welcome to the visitors who come to our services, given that well over ninety percent of the people who join us in worship are visitors to the college and to the chapel. At the beginning of the service you can see them and identify them easily; from the moment they walk into the chapel their heads go up and their jaws go down. Sometimes they sidle up and whisper confidentially that they are realizing a dream that they have cherished for decades and have traveled halfway around the world to visit us and worship with us. That is a colossal responsibility. We have much to live up to. What we have to offer as our gift is God's gift to them. If we get it wrong—if we make them feel that the place is cold and unfriendly and unwelcoming, little more than a concert hall, and that they are basically there on sufferance, then we have got it horribly wrong, and we may never get another chance. Sometimes we do get it wrong, and they tell us. It is searingly painful, because you cannot say, "Please come back next week and we'll try and do better." They have gone back to Sydney by then. Our responsibility weighs heavily.

Jesus' uncompromising attitude to those who fail to offer a welcome is recorded in all three synoptic gospels: Matthew 10, Mark 6, and Luke 9. "If you are not welcomed in a town," he tells the disciples, "shake its dust from off your feet and move on." And, in Matthew, for good measure, there is added that "it will be more bearable for Sodom and Gomorrah on the day of judgment" (10:15, NIV) than for that particular town. We have been clearly warned.

With opportunities, therefore, come responsibilities. New acquaintances mean new effort, new links that sometimes need serious and time-consuming work if they are to last and to grow in the chain of human interaction. It is not for nothing that we speak of links of a chain being forged. The imagery of iron is an apt one, but the sad truth is that even such institutions as the church have found ways over the centuries to make certain groups of people feel unwelcome and marginalized. Women are now only beginning to take their full and rightful place in the church's hierarchy after some exceedingly bitter confrontations. Two weeks ago it was decided that there really should be no barrier—what I heard referred to as "the stained-glass ceiling"—to prevent women from becoming bishops. Alleluia! At the same time, the church is making a heroically excellent job of fudging the whole issue of homosexuality. I heard a priest say on the radio recently that no one in any affirmed, committed, monogamous homosexual relationship should be offered the sacraments of baptism or the sacrament of the eucharist. How welcoming is that? How imaginative is that?

In our eucharistic prayer we say, "He opened wide his arms for us on the cross." Open arms is a gesture of defiance: defiance of the powers of death. It is a gesture of resignation: resignation to the will of God. It is also a gesture of welcome: welcome to all who turn and run with similarly outstretched arms to the arms of God's warm embrace. Let us, with similarly open arms, offer our own welcome to the stranger we meet as well as to the people close to us. For who knows? We may, thereby, be entertaining angels unawares.

Let us pray.

Heavenly Father, we give you thanks for what we have been given—the endless opportunities we have to meet new people, to embrace them into our circle of acquaintance. We pray that we may not ever be so blinkered as to try to stamp the pattern of our agenda onto them, but that we may always be channels, crystal and clear-flowing, of your love for them. Oh God, make the doors of our hearts and our churches wide enough to receive all who need human love and fellowship, but narrow enough to shut out all envy, pride, and strife. Make their thresholds smooth enough to be no stumbling block to children nor to straying feet, but strong enough to turn back the tempter's power. Lord our God, make the doors of our churches and our hearts gateways to your eternal kingdom for the sake of Christ our Lord. Amen.

Public Worship

What's that part about the lump of clay
tryin' not to be a pot,
when all it has to do is let go
and the potter does the rest?
And there they stand,
readin' from the book,
when all it wants to do
is tell itself,
if they would only let it.

Louisville, Ky.
1991

8

The Goodness of True Worship

Harry Lee Poe

In recent years, for the past fifteen years or so, a controversy has raged among many Christians over style of worship. It has even been referred to as "the worship wars." Many places of worship now house the symbols of the worship wars. Many have video projectors hanging from the ceiling in the center of the room. Now who would ever have thought of that forty years ago? It is a different kind of ornament than we once knew, but this kind of change is not unique to our generation. The church has gone through this kind of change every few generations; it is nothing unusual. Every few generations for the past two thousand years, part of the church experiences a sudden change in the style and manner of worship, while another part of the church holds to an earlier tradition.

Thinking about worship, I would like to look at the twelfth chapter of Romans. I will not expound the entire chapter, but I will focus on selected verses and point to blocks of text as we go through. I use the *New International Version,* but I learned this passage in the *King James:* "I beseech you therefore, brethren, by the mercies of God, that you present your bodies a living sacrifice, holy, acceptable to God, which is your reasonable service" (Rom. 12:1). The *New International Version* translates that word "service" as "worship." We use these two words interchangeably. We say, "We're going to have the service at eleven o'clock," or, "We're going to have the evening service at six o'clock." When we say "the service," we mean "the worship."

Spiritual Worship

One of the things the apostle Paul makes clear in the twelfth chapter of Romans is that the worship of God does not primarily take place in a "worship building" or a "worship room." The worship of God does not primarily involve songs. It does not primarily involve preaching. It does not primarily involve praying. For many people, the idea of worship involves a particular place, particular time, ritual, pattern, or other familiar activities that a group does together. I think we have this idea because, in the Old Testament, God laid out specific commandments that had to be followed related to serving him. Service involved a sacrificial system that could only be carried out at one place on the face of the earth—that was the temple in Jerusalem. It could only be led by the priesthood descended from Aaron. Everything about it was laid out, including the clothes that were worn by the priests and how absolutely everything about the ceremonies would take place. God made these commands about worship, and then he turned right around and declared through the prophets that he hated it all (Isa. 1:11–17; Am. 5:21–24; Zech. 7:4–10). He hated the sacrifices. He hated the solemn assemblies. He hated the festivals and the feasts. He hated it all. His response seems very strange, because God is the one who commanded them to do it. On the other hand, God's regard for worship practices was not a new thing for the children of Israel. He had expressed himself on the matter long before Moses or the Law.

If we go back to the very beginning of the Bible, we find the first worship war was between Cain and Abel. God accepted one sacrifice, but did not accept the other. At the very beginning God explained the problem with worship. There was a problem with the human heart. That is the ugly, little problem.

When Jesus Christ came, he met a woman of Samaria one day by a well in the heat of the day. John tells the story in the fourth chapter of his gospel. The Samaritan woman posed the religious question that so many people use to put off the consideration of the claims of the gospel, the claims of Jesus Christ our Lord. Rather than dealing with the reality of God, they want to focus on who does it right, the Methodists or the Baptists, and get sidetracked into issues of worship.

She asked who worshiped rightly, her family who worshiped on the mountain in Samaria, or the Jews and the family of Jesus who worshiped at the temple in Jerusalem. Do you remember his answer? "God is a Spirit: and they that worship him must worship him in spirit and in truth" (Jn. 4:24, KJV). That is what Paul is talking about in the twelfth chapter of Romans. What is your reasonable worship? Reasonable worship involves presenting yourself as a living sacrifice to God. Other than that, the New Testament says very, very little about worship. It would make it easy if the new covenant laid out all the rules about all the rituals. Then you would know when you were doing it right and when you were doing it wrong. Jesus does not allow us the comfort of legalism and prescription: "They that worship him must worship him in spirit and in truth."

Paul is talking about Jesus' view of worship in the twelfth chapter of Romans. He goes on to say, "And be not conformed to this world: but be ye transformed by the renewing of your mind" (Rom. 12:2a, KJV). Now I will switch to the New International Version. Instead of going along with the crowd, we need to be thinking constantly about changing ourselves. If you do that, "Then you will be able to test and approve what God's will is—his good, pleasing and perfect will" (Rom. 12:2b, NIV).

Recognizing What Is Good

What is the will of God? Notice what Paul says about it. First of all, it is good (v. 2). The will of God is good. Throughout the rest of this chapter Paul lays out how you go about not being conformed to the world and how you go about understanding the will of God. The idea of goodness is one of the key terms found in this passage and the rest of the chapter. How do you know if your worship is true? How do you know what constitutes beautiful worship? What makes for good worship? The idea of good worship—goodness—appears several more times in this chapter.

If there is anything good, Paul tells the Philippians in the fourth chapter of Philippians, then think about that. Unfortunately, people have a problem knowing what is good and what is not good. We say all sorts of things are good. That pie my wife makes is really good. I bought a wrench one time; it was a good wrench. We use the word *good* in many different ways. That is a good light in the ceiling because it does what it is supposed to do. Sometimes we say, "Well, I am basically a good person." How do we use the word *good* then? Someone came up to Jesus once and asked, "Good teacher,…what must I do to inherit eternal life?" (Mk. 10:17b, NIV). Jesus stopped him cold in his tracks and replied, "Why do you call me good?…No one is good—except God alone" (Mk. 10:18, NIV).

When I first learned to pray, I was taught to pray, "God is great, God is good." Only God is good. Whatever God does is good. Now here's the trick. If only God is good, then how do we explain it when we come across something in this world that is good?—and there is a lot in this world that is good. Don't let anyone ever tell you that there is nothing in the world that is good. If they say that, then they are saying that God does not exist. We know from reading the first chapter of the Bible that everything God made was good. Everything. He planned it, he did it, and what he did is good. So whenever in the course of life you come across something good, you will know that God has been at work doing something.

Sometimes God does good things in spite of us, because he is so much bigger than we are. God is so much bigger than our frailty. Remember that when the brothers of Joseph sold him into slavery down to Egypt, they intended it for evil. But remember what the Bible says? "God intended it for good" (Gen. 50:20,

NIV). God can take the worst situations in the world and turn them into good. Why? Because he's God. As Paul had already explained to the Romans a few chapters earlier, "In all things God works for the good of those who love him, who have been called according to his purpose" (Rom. 8:28, NIV).

The Gift That Enables Transformation

So how do we transform ourselves? The first thing Paul tells us in verses three through eight is that before God expects us to do anything, he does something first. Paul prefaces his explanation with the remark, "For by the grace given me…" (Rom. 12:3a, NIV). He starts off by saying that God did something in his life first. God does not expect us to change before he will be gracious to us. Instead, he bestows his grace upon us when we are unworthy of acceptance. God is the one who takes the initiative in changing us. We cannot change ourselves. It is the Holy Spirit of God who indwells us when we trust him who changes us from glory unto glory (2 Cor. 3:17–18).

Let's go back to the woman at the well. When Jesus said, "They that worship him must worship him in spirit and in truth," do you remember what he was talking to her about at the time? They were talking about water. They were talking about being thirsty, and he told her that he could give her a water that when she drank it, she would never thirst again. This living water would become a well. Not just a well—a fountain, a stream, flowing constantly. This water is not something you can collect or store in a cistern; it is a flowing stream. He was speaking of the Holy Spirit of God. You cannot change yourself. You cannot save yourself. You cannot deal with the problem of sin in your life. Only God does it, and he does it when he himself comes into our lives by his Holy Spirit and changes us. Do not be conformed to the world. Why? You no longer have to be conformed to the world anymore. You can be transformed. Do not submit yourself in slavery to the world once you have been set free (Rom. 6—8). Be transformed.

So Paul makes the big point in verses three through eight that when the Spirit of God comes in, he gives us power. Remember, he told Timothy he hadn't been given a spirit of fear" (2 Tim. 1:7a). Fear does not come from God. What kind of spirit did God give us? One of power, one of love, one of a sound mind (2 Tim. 1:7b). These same three ideas come together also in this passage, because the idea of the mind being changed involves the one who gives us a sound mind. Have you ever been really confused, and what you most wanted God to do was calm you down so you could see things and think through things clearly? That is the gift he gives: a sound mind. He also gives the power to do whatever he asks us to do. We do not have the power in our own strength, but he gives us the power to do it.

The Fruit of Transformation

After Paul makes clear the work of God, he then moves on to what it means to be transformed. Notice verse nine: "Love must be sincere" (Rom. 12:9a, NIV). Many people talk about the apostle John as the apostle of love—the one who wrote the gospel of John and the three letters and the book of Revelation—because love is such an important theme in his writings. We can think of John 3:16—"For God so loved the world…" . But I think an even stronger case can be made for Paul as the apostle of love, because he was preoccupied with the love of Christ. Wasn't it Paul who wrote that thirteenth chapter of First Corinthians that so many people want read at their weddings, about the meaning of love? In the fifth chapter of Romans Paul says that God's love is poured into our hearts by the Holy Spirit. A person who may have never had the capacity for love in their natural state suddenly experiences the love of God and has the capacity to love. When the Holy Spirit comes, God, who is love, saves us and gives us a capacity we never really had before in its fullness. So let love be sincere. The presence of true love is absolutely critical to the worship of God.

Then he moves on to how love relates to goodness: "Hate what is evil; cling to what is good" (Rom. 12:9b, NIV). God makes a clear distinction between evil and goodness, because God himself is goodness. There is no gray here. It is not vague. There *is* such a thing as evil. It is not just a matter of opinion.

There really is badness and wickedness in the world, and we are to recognize it. How do we recognize it? We recognize it the same way that bank clerks learn to recognize a true bill from a counterfeit. You handle the real stuff; you spend a lot of time with the real stuff. You feel the real stuff. Then when the counterfeit comes along, you recognize it for what it is. You spend time with the Lord himself, and then you recognize evil and wickedness when it creeps up on you. Jesus warned us that evil does not come creeping up with a big wave and a flag, saying, "Hey, I'm wicked and evil." No. Evil comes as a wolf in sheep's clothing. It comes with soft, beautiful words.

Harry Potter is a recent literary creation, and there is some question about whether Harry Potter is satanic or just fantasy, like the Wizard of Oz. He is a little boy wizard. One thing that strikes me about the Harry Potter stories is that in an age when postmodernity has made everything relative—there is no right, there is no wrong, it's all a matter of personal opinion—in an age in which there are no absolutes anymore—no truth, no falsehood; it's all a matter of personal opinion—in the Harry Potter stories there is good and evil. Here is a case of children learning to recognize evil and to name it. It does not have to be an Adolf Hitler to be evil, or in Harry Potter's case the wicked wizard, Lord Voldemort. The children in the story learn to recognize evil in other school children. They learn to recognize it at an early age, where it may take a very simple form. They learn to recognize it in teachers, in relatives, in their friends, and most important of all, they learn to recognize it in themselves. Ah, there's the trick. You can recognize it in another—do you see the speck in your brother's eye but you don't recognize the beam in your own eye, Jesus asks? That is the problem. It is not just a matter of hating what is evil out there. It primarily involves hating what is evil in here, within myself. That is the greatest obstacle to my worship of God.

In this passage between verses nine and twenty-one, Paul rattles off one right after another, coming fast and faster, what it looks like for love to be sincere and how to do what is good:

> Be devoted to one another in brotherly love. Honor one another above yourselves. Never be lacking in zeal, but keep your spiritual fervor, serving the Lord. Be joyful in hope, patient in affliction, faithful in prayer. Share with God's people who are in need. Practice hospitality. (Rom. 12:10–13, NIV)

Some passages in Paul's letters are very difficult to understand; even Peter thought so (2 Pet. 3:15–16), and theologians for two thousand years have been pondering the depth of some of these very profound passages. But the most important passages are crystal clear. What does it mean to practice hospitality? That is not very hard to understand. It only takes two words to explain: practice hospitality. There is nothing vague, deep, or hard to understand about that, is there? When we get down to the real crux of what it means to worship God, to render our reasonable service to him, not to be conformed to the world but to be transformed, it really is pretty plain.

Paul goes on to say, "Bless those who persecute you" (Rom. 12:14a, NIV). One of the problems with things being plain is that we do not really want them to be plain. I do not want to bless those who persecute me. I want to curse those who persecute me. There again, somebody's got a problem. Those who persecute me have a problem, but the Lord does not want me to add to my affliction the same wickedness as the one who persecutes me.

Paul continues, "Rejoice with those who rejoice" (Rom. 12:15a, NIV). That is a little easier. I like to do that one. "Mourn with those who mourn" (Rom. 12:15b, NIV). Notice how some of these statements seem to echo the Sermon on the Mount? Jesus said, "Blessed are those who mourn, for they will be comforted" (Mt. 5:4, NIV). Who will do the comforting? Christ has assigned that responsibility to his church. Oh, the Holy Spirit is the Great Comforter, but we are the body of Christ that has the responsibility to give the physical embrace. That is what brothers and sisters in the Lord do for one another. That is the reasonable service.

Again Paul says, "Live in harmony with one another" (Rom. 12:16a, NIV). There he goes again, meddling. "Do not be proud, but be willing to associate with people of low position. Do not be conceited" (Rom. 12:16b, NIV). Notice how it only takes a few words to echo the character of Jesus Christ.

And again Paul says, "Do not repay anyone evil for evil. Be careful to do what is right in the eyes of everybody. If it is possible, as far as it depends on you, live at peace with everyone" (Rom. 12:17–18). Paul makes an important qualification here, and I think it is one of the great graces that God permitted the apostle Paul to reveal to Christian people. We find that important teaching, "Live at peace with everyone," but to it is added the qualification: "If it is possible, as far as it depends on you." There are some people with whom you cannot live peacefully. There are some people who will absolutely refuse to get along with you. It is not your fault, and the Bible makes it clear: "as far as it depends upon you." Go as far as you can to get along, but we are not responsible for how people respond to us. Leave the final word to God:

> Do not take revenge, my friends, but leave room for God's wrath' for it is written: "It is mine to avenge; I will repay," says the Lord. On the contrary:
> "If your enemy is hungry, feed him;
>   if he's thirsty, give him something to drink.
> In doing this, you will heap burning coals on his
>   head." (Rom. 12:19—20, NIV)

Conclusion

In the final verse of this passage, Paul returns to the idea of goodness: "Do not be overcome by evil, but overcome evil with good" (Rom. 12:21, NIV). What is good? The great series of books, *The Lord of the Rings,* tells the story of a ring of power—a demonic device, evil to the core. One of the things that we learn is that you cannot use this ring of power for a good purpose. If you try to use it, because it is evil, you will become the slave to the evil. It is essentially what Paul is saying here, and here is essentially where J. R. R. Tolkien got the idea. What does it look like to be overcome by evil? It does not mean someone has done an evil thing to you and defeated you. The world did an evil thing to Jesus Christ—nailed him to a cross and killed him. Was he overcome by evil? No. In fact, through that seeming tragedy he tells us that he overcame the world. Remember what he said? "Be of good cheer; I have overcome the world" (Jn. 16:33, KJV). How? He died. Instead, to be overcome by evil means to try to use evil to accomplish your purpose. In so doing you have made yourself a slave to it, and evil has overcome you. Evil has won the victory. You can only overcome evil with good. And what is goodness? Wrong question. Instead, we should ask, *Who* is goodness? The Lord himself is goodness.

Do not be conformed to this world. Be transformed. Cooperate with the Spirit of God who comes into you when you trust Jesus Christ. Remember what he told his disciples that last night with them after the supper? He told them that it was good for them that he was leaving. If he did not leave, the Spirit of Truth would not come. When the Spirit comes and makes his home in the disciples, however, Jesus explained that his father and he would make their homes in them as well (Jn. 14:15–23). The very power that created this universe dwells lovingly and richly within the heart of every person who trusts Jesus.

God is a Spirit. They that worship him must worship him in spirit and in truth. True worship manifests the goodness of the presence of God in our lives.

Can God Talk?

Can God talk?
Is God capable of communicating on a level
as high as we?
Or, is God a lower form of life
made in the image of the mollusk or amoeba?
Has God transcended communication,
like my students who emit low guttural noises
from expressionless faces?
Perhaps he cannot talk at all.
He could be a deaf mute.
Instead of the highest form of life,
what if God were the lowest?

Union University
Jackson, Tenn.
September 2004

Marrying Talent to
Christlike Character

Vishal Mangalwadi

TEXT: 1 Samuel 16:7

The theme of our presentations is "Making All Things New: The Good, the True, and the Beautiful in the Twenty-first Century." The first point I would like to make is that it is not really our responsibility to make all things new. This is part of a statement from Jesus Christ, who said, "Behold, I make all things new" (Rev. 21:5, KJV). The Bible is a great story, a long story, a meta-narrative in which the hero is God himself. He creates, and then he has a problem. He has created people with intellect and will, and they have chosen to rebel against him. They have spoiled his perfect and good and beautiful creation. What is God going to do about it? He is involved in a mission, the triumph of good over evil, and that is the great story. God is redeeming his creation, and that gives us hope. We are invited to participate with him—to become new creatures and the instruments of his mission to redeem and restore all things. That is the interactive story in which we begin to participate in God's mission to restore all things.

Now what are we to do? I am not the savior. He is the Savior, but what is my role? That is what I would like us to consider. I would like to propose that our role in the twenty-first century is to marry our talent to Christlike character. That is really the message that I would like to give: marrying talent to Christlike character.

Samuel was a prophet at the end of the period of the Judges. The Judges ruled Israel for about 350 or 400 years. During this period Israel had no kings until Samuel anointed Saul. Saul turned out just like the kings around Israel, as God had warned; and Samuel was quite upset. Then the Lord said to Samuel:

> "How long will you mourn for Saul, [the first king whom Samuel had anointed to be the king], since I have rejected him as king over Israel? Fill your horn with oil and be on your way; I am sending you to Jesse of Bethlehem. I have chosen one of his sons to be king."
>
> But Samuel said, "How can I go? Saul will hear about it and kill me."
>
> The LORD said, "Take a heifer with you and say, 'I have come to sacrifice to the Lord.' Invite Jesse to the sacrifice, and I will show you what to do. You are to anoint for me the one I indicate."
>
> Samuel did what the LORD said. When he arrived at Bethlehem, the elders of the town trembled when they met him. They asked, "Do you come in peace?"
>
> Samuel replied, "Yes, in peace; I have come to sacrifice to the LORD. Consecrate yourselves, and come to the sacrifice with me." (1 Sam. 16:1—5a, NIV)

Now the elders are worried that God has rejected Saul. "Have you come here to cause an insurrection? Are you going to bring trouble upon us? Saul will march in if you are trying to organize rebellion." So he is really doing a sacrifice.

When they [Jesse's family] arrived, Samuel saw Eliab [the first son, the eldest son] and thought,

"Surely the LORD's anointed stands here before the LORD."

But the LORD said to Samuel, "Do not consider his appearance or his height, for I have rejected him. The LORD does not look at the things man looks at. Man looks at the outward appearance, but the LORD looks at the heart." (1 Sam. 16:6—7, NIV)

I would like to focus on this last verse.

Samuel is impressed by the external appearance, the beauty of this man—how handsome he is, how tall he is, how good-looking he is. And God says, "Don't look at the outward, because I don't really look at the outward. I look at the heart—at the character."

Many of us have read this passage to mean that God is not really bothered about physical beauty. God is not really bothered about talents and arts and skills and things that we do on the canvas or with mud, or metals—what we create. He looks at the character. Well, that is actually not what is happening here. I want to suggest that what is happening here is indeed the marriage of talent and character.

The passage goes on to say that finally David is brought. The other six sons are all rejected, and then David is brought. He is a young teenager. Jesse, the father, sent a messenger to bring in David. He was ruddy, with a fine appearance and handsome features. He was good-looking. Physical beauty is, indeed, good, and it takes a lot of hard work to look beautiful. Some of us do not look as beautiful as we should because we are not willing to do that hard work.

Now David is good-looking, but he is not simply good-looking. He is very talented. The chapter continues to say that Saul has become evil. He is possessed by an evil spirit that torments him. He loses his sanity. Since they do not have medication, they want to bring a musician to play for Saul to calm him down. One of the servants suggests, "I have seen a son of Jesse of Bethlehem who knows how to play the harp. He is a brave man and a warrior. He speaks well, is a fine-looking man, and the LORD is with him" (1 Sam. 16:18, NIV).

So here is David, a shepherd boy. He has been anointed, but has gone back to look after sheep. He is a musician—a very good musician, also a brave man and a warrior. He has skills with musical instruments and, as it turns out, he is a great poet. In fact, there has been no poet in the whole of human history who has been read more, and memorized more, than David. And he plays very well. He is a very talented man. He is also a very brave man who can take on lions and bears and Goliaths as a very skillful warrior—a very talented man.

The reason he is chosen, however, is because he is a man after God's own heart. To be a king, you have to have talent. Saul himself is an outstanding man. The phrase "head and shoulders above everyone else" comes from Saul. When he was chosen by lot to be the king, he was hiding in the midst of the baggage, and when they found him and he stood up in the hall, he was "higher than any of the people from his shoulders and upward" (1 Sam. 10:23b, KJV). He is outstanding, not only in his physical appearance, but also in his military strategy. He became the king after he liberated Jabesh Gilead from the Philistines. He fought. He is a talented man. His problem is with his heart—with his character. He has been rejected. The story of his rejection is very important, because that summarizes what had been going on in Israel for 350 years at least. Samuel, the prophet, was a young boy when Samson died. Samson was a highly talented man, but addicted to pleasure. He became driven by his lust. He became spiritually blind before he became physically blind and was killed. Eli, who mentored Samuel, became spiritually blind. His sons were looting the temple, taking God's portion. They were raping the women who came to offer sacrifices in the tabernacle. God said to Eli that because you do not honor me, and because you have rejected my word, I am rejecting your whole family.

When the book of Samuel opens, Samuel is a young man. We read that in those days the word of God was very rare. When

God spoke to Samuel, Samuel did not know that it was God speaking. Samuel kept going to Eli and asking, "Did you call me?" He was like most people—"How can God speak? Can God speak?" Moses saw a bush burning and went to see what was going on there. Why wasn't it consumed? And this bush started talking to him. Can a bush speak? Was it God's word, or was it his imagination? Well, Moses questioned it, he tested it, and he was convinced that it was God speaking. It turned out that everything God described in that encounter later happened. Moses did not want to go back to Egypt, but he obeyed and he saw. God said that Moses would bring the slaves out of Egypt, and that he would come back to the mountain to worship him. Now, the mountain of Sinai was not en route from Egypt to Israel, but Moses came back and met with God again. The whole community met with God.

Does God speak? Eli learned that he does. Samuel learned that he does. When Samuel became a prophet, everything he said came true. There is a wonderful phrase for this: "not one word failed." So God does speak, and God does speak through his prophets. He even spoke to Saul. Saul was anointed king. Why, then, did God reject Saul? In 1 Samuel 13 we discover that Saul was rejected because he had been told to wait for Samuel to offer sacrifice before going to a war. But his army began deserting him so Saul went ahead and offered the sacrifice himself. Samuel then arrived. He was very upset and declared, "You have rejected God's word; God is rejecting you." Why? Why is he so upset? Is he so upset because "only I can offer sacrifice as priest?" No. When Israel asked for a king, Samuel saw that this would mean totalitarianism. A Jewish king would not be any better than a pharaoh.

Unless God's word binds a king's authority, the king will be oppressive. Samuel was not pleased, because in asking for a king, Israel rejected God as king. But he gave them a king anyway. It could work if the king submitted to God's word. Part of God's law was that the Levitical priest would offer the sacrifices. Saul disregarded God's word. He was already the political, military, and judicial leader. He was taking over the office of the religious leader as well. He centralized power in himself. Samuel says, "Uh-oh. This is terrible. This is going to turn Israel into an oppressive society. Israel has got to be a nation where the word of God is supreme. What you are rejecting is God's word; therefore, God will reject you."

Saul is finally rejected in 1 Samuel 15 because Samuel told him that when he destroyed the Amalekites, he was to dedicate the spoils to the LORD. Saul won a great victory, but he and his soldiers kept the best sheep and other animals for themselves. Samuel came and asked, "What's going on here? You were told to devote these things to the Lord." Saul replied, "Oh, we are keeping these to offer as sacrifices to your God." Does God want bribes? Or does he want obedience? Samuel told Saul, "Since you have rejected the word of God, you are going to be rejected." So a common problem for Samson, Eli, Eli's sons, and Saul was that they were very talented people who did not submit their hearts to God's word; therefore, they were rejected.

David is chosen because he is a very talented man who cultivated his talent. He was not talented because he went to an art school, music school, drama school, or film school—he is a shepherd. David saw that God had called him to be a shepherd: "If I'm to be like God, then God must be a shepherd." In trying to be a Godlike shepherd, he cultivated his talent: "If God were a shepherd, what would he do to these sheep? That's what I must do." As a result of his desire to become like God, we have the beautiful poetry of Psalm 23 from a shepherd. David's poem has blessed billions of people throughout history.

In being faithful to who you are, if God takes care of every sheep, then what am I to do when a lion comes and tries to take my sheep? Well, if God has called me to be a shepherd, he has called me to defend the sheep. Then I have got to take on the lions. That is where David learned his bravery; that is where he learned his faith; that is where he learned his war. He never went to a military academy, but as a shepherd, being faithful in what God called him to do, and his character was cultivated into Christlikeness because of his obedience.

Why do I call it Christlike character? Because Jesus is the real Davidic king—a king like David. What is the heart of Jesus? What shaped his character? In 1 Corinthians 15:3—4, Paul summarizes the gospel. What is of first importance? Poetry, music, film, arts? Paul says, "I communicated to you that which is of absolute primary importance, and that is that Jesus Christ died for our sins according to the scriptures, was buried, and rose again the third day according to the scriptures. This is the primary thing."

We take it to mean that Jesus died for our sins and rose again for our salvation; that's the gospel. In that one phrase, however, Paul twice repeats that Jesus did this "according to the scriptures." What does that mean? What it means is that Jesus died to obey and to fulfill the scriptures? He did not want to die. Peter said to him, "Don't die." Jesus said, "Of course, I can call twelve legions of angels; I don't have to die. But how, then, will the scriptures be fulfilled? I'm dying because, 'It is written.'"

Was Jesus Lord? C. S. Lewis argued that he was. What was he like? He was a man who didn't just die by the word of God, but also lived by the word of God. When Satan came to tempt him, he said, "Turn these stones into bread." Jesus answered, "No. For it is written that man shall not live by bread alone but by every word that proceeds from the mouth of God" (Lk. 4:4 paraphrased). Jesus is committed to what is written. He is not a postmodernist!

God speaks. God has spoken. Israel had been having problems, and those problems are described in the book of Judges. Israel had become an awful and ugly society, like India, like Ukraine, like Russia. What was needed was a king who would set his heart to obey God's word, and that king is Jesus. He lived by the word of God. Doesn't he have a living relationship with a living God? Wasn't he baptized with the Holy Spirit? Doesn't he commune with the Holy Spirit? Why does he need the written word? Are there absolutes?

I agree that there are no absolutes in arts, but what do we have? What we have is Romans 12:1–2—"Do not be conformed to this world, but be ye transformed by the renewing of your mind, so that you might test and approve and discern the will of God" (paraphrased). Isn't God's will plainly stated in the scriptures? Yes and no. "Thou shall not commit a murder; thou shall not kill." That's an absolute. It is stated clearly. But is that God's highest will for me? No. His highest will for me is to love my neighbor. But what does that mean? Does that mean planting flowers for him? Watering her flowers? Mowing his lawn? As your mind is renewed, you don't need absolutes. Absolutes are the bottom line. You need maturity, perfection, so that you might know God's will.

Are there limits? Are there absolutes? No. You need to become perfect as your father in Heaven is perfect, to be transformed by God's word. So, is Jesus living by God's word? Yes. He takes the word of God so literally that he is willing to give his life for it. He laid down his life. That's what shapes character. The highly talented young Jedi master became Darth Vader because good was only an opinion. It was not absolute for him. He believed that evil is only the dark side of the same force; it is not against God. It is not against God's will. If we water down the authority of the word of God and do not commit ourselves to the word of God, our talent will turn us into Darth Vader. What is happening in the West now in the twenty-first century is exactly what happened during the Renaissance. Scholasticism had collapsed, which meant the method of knowing truth had collapsed—trying to understand revelation through Greek logic did not work.

If we cannot know truth, substance does not matter; only style matters. Aesthetics matters, but the church that patronized art became the most corrupt church in history. That is why Erasmus called for reforms. We can decide to cultivate great talent because we cannot know truth; therefore, we go for art. You can have great talent, which can become diabolical. It does not matter if you are the pope or if you are a bishop or if you are a theologian. What is needed is a heart that is submitted to God's word.

In conclusion, what does it mean for me to partner with God in making all things beautiful, all things new, all things good and true? We have understood Samuel simplistically if we think that God does not look at talent and at externals, but only looks at the heart. No—he very much looked at David's talents, his abilities, his skills, his practice of what he believed. The important thing, indeed, is marrying that talent to a character—Christlike character—a character that is dedicated to obeying the authority of the word of God. This is not an aesthetic thing, but is a continuing transformation of the mind so that I might keep discerning what the mind and the will of God is. Then I will not be legalistic in my art, but be liberated to fantasize, to imagine, and to create beautiful things.

The Great Santee Swamp

A snowy plane of egrets' feathers carpeted the swamp.
The gondolas of fibrous plumage sailed the quiet slough,
isolated from the Santee River channel's flow.
Within the darkened water course, thick draped with
    Spanish moss,
protected by the phalanx formed of water, trees, and brush,
dimly shown the feathers, like a sanctuary's lamp.

Silently our boatman moved the john boat through the glade.
The ruffled whiteness floating on the surface formed a cloud
on which we seemed suspended for the moment from the
    world.
As though a massive moccasin, whose mouth of cotton white,
had opened wide its jaws to satisfy its appetite:
the whiteness was the pale of bones, the pallor of the dead.

The secret mausoleum reeked of ruin and decay.
Where fallen oaks and poplar trees lay rotting in the mire,
stretched out like mummies in a tomb, the feathers formed
    a shroud.
The death and spoilage of ten thousand years remains to
    dwell
within the boundaries where life deposited its shell,
where waters fouled by humankind are cleansed and
    purged away.

What providential wisdom uses death to foster life?
Devouring the putrescence that poisons as it goes,
the swamp grows ancient while it heals the gentle waters' flow.
What subtlety of purposes would transform life again
from carrion and vileness in a sepulcher's domain
to pure and sparkling clarity, embodiment of light?

Simpsonville, Ky.
March 1986

10

The Network of Minds /
The Network of Grace

Joseph Pearce

TEXT: John 9:25, 39–41

I was brought to Christ through reading some of the great writers of what I call the Christian cultural revival of the twentieth century. I include names such as G. K. Chesterton, Hilaire Belloc, T. S. Eliot, C. S. Lewis, J. R. R. Tolkien, Evelyn Waugh, and others. I became interested in that whole period because I began to realize that none of these people were an island. They did not exist in isolation. They did not exist in a vacuum. They influenced others and were being influenced by others. As part of my research for *Literary Converts,* one of my books that is basically a history of this whole Christian cultural revival in the twentieth century, I interviewed Barbara Reynolds. Barbara Reynolds lives in Cambridge. She was a great friend of Dorothy L. Sayers, another one of these leading figures in the Christian cultural revival. Dorothy L. Sayers died halfway through translating *Paradise* from Dante's *Divine Comedy,* having already translated the first two books. Barbara Reynolds took over—she is a great Italian scholar—and finished the translation.

When I was interviewing her, she suddenly said to me, "this Christian cultural revival was like a network of minds energizing each other." That struck me, and I quoted it in my book. But it has also struck me since then that it is not just a network of minds. It is a network of grace that does the energizing with which the minds cooperate.

So how did the likes of Chesterton and Lewis save a miserable sinner like me? And I was a miserable sinner. When I was undergoing instruction to be received into the Catholic Church, the priest asked me to write an essay, which is very unusual. It is not usually the way that people are received into the church. He knew that I was a writer, that I had written, and had things published, so he thought it might be the appropriate way. He said, "write an essay on your conversion." I could only think of beginning it with the lines of a very famous hymn: "Amazing grace, how sweet the sound that saved a wretch like me. / I once was lost but now am found. Was blind, but now I see." Because I was blind. I was blinded by prejudice, I was blinded by hatred, I was blinded by bitterness, I was blinded by ignorance.

I was brought up basically as an agnostic. Technically I was an Anglican in the sense that I was christened, or baptized, but only because it was a *faux pas,* shall we say, not to be christened. Only common people do not christen their children. After that we never went to church except for weddings. I was not allowed to go to funerals when I was a child, so I only went to weddings. There was no prayer life. I was essentially an agnostic. I was never an atheist. I never thought dogmatically that God did not exist. Quite frankly, I did not know and did not care. He was not important. There were more important things in life than God.

I was, however, brought up to be very anti-Catholic, and this is a little bit difficult now because to give this testimony I have to mention my father, who passed away on Tuesday morning. My father was very anti-Catholic. This is something about English culture that we need to understand. November 5, Guy Fawkes Night, we still celebrate in commemoration of the burning of Guy Fawkes for a papist plot in 1605. People make an effigy of Guy Fawkes, put him on top of the bonfire, and burn him. This is still done all over the country. In some towns, such as Lewes in Sussex, they still burn an effigy of the pope and also an effigy of whoever is particularly unpopular that year in politics. I went there in the mid-1980s, and the pope shared the honor of being burned with Ronald Reagan. At that time I approved heartily of both burnings.

So I was brought up with this anti-Catholicism. My mother's mother was from Ireland. None of the children were brought up Catholic, but she was obviously Catholic. When she died my mother brought home her rosary beads. My father came home one night when I was a young child and said, "We're not having these papist beads in the house," and threw them out the window.

At the age of fifteen, the lost soul that I was, I got involved with extremist politics—white supremacist politics in England. I joined an organization called The National Front that believed in compulsory repatriation of all nonwhites to their lands of ethnic origin. I became a very prominent member of that organization. I became the youngest ever member of its governing body at the age of, I think, seventeen. I edited its first youth journal with the rather charming pseudonym of "Bulldog." That group was virulent in its racism, deliberately so because it was adopting the Trotskyite approach. What we had to do was to make society unstable so it would all collapse into revolution. The Trotskyites believe you do that by fomenting class war. We believed you did it by fomenting race war. This magazine that I edited was actually intended to stir up enmity, hatred, between the races.

In 1981 I was charged under the Race Relations Act with publishing material likely to incite racial hatred. Then in the beginning of 1982 I was sentenced to six months in prison for editing that magazine. I came out as resolute in my racism as ever, considered myself a political prisoner when I was in prison. When I came out, I carried on as before, considering myself very clever. I did not call myself Joseph Pearce, as editor; I called myself "Captain Truth." I thought they would not be able to prosecute me. Well, the British police force may not be the smartest people in the world, but they are not that silly. One morning, at about four o'clock in the morning, my house was raided. They found all the evidence they needed. I was duly charged again with publishing material likely to incite racial hatred, and I was sentenced this time to twelve months in prison.

I should say, by the way, that if being involved in a white supremacist organization was not bad enough, I also got myself very heavily involved with terrorist organizations. I became very involved with the Loyalist paramilitaries in Northern Ireland. My anti-Catholicism now took political form. I detested the IRA and sang songs that I will not sing now that were very, very, anti-Catholic. I joined the Orange Order, which is a secret society for Protestants only. In fact, not really for Protestants only—for anybody who does not like Catholics, because I was not a Protestant and one of my friends who was an avowed atheist was a member. That was fine. As long as you did not like Catholics you could join. You did not have to be Protestant. But Catholics were not allowed to join. I also got involved with the UDA, the Ulster Defense Association, and the UVF, the Ulster Volunteer Force, who are paramilitary groups, basically fighting a tit-for-tat murder campaign against the IRA.

The difference during my second prison sentence was that things had changed. Between the first prison sentence and the second prison sentence, I began to read some of these great writers that I mentioned. You can imagine that if you join an organization like the one I joined, when you are fifteen, there is not all that much in your brain. That was about the time that I started liking to read books. I became a bibliophile and ate up and consumed all of this racist nonsense that they gave me. By the time I was nineteen I could have argued with anybody from a racist perspective, because I had read all these books on the subject, and had read nothing else.

In the midst of all this, lots of violence was involved in the lifestyle—particularly with the extreme Left, with the communists. If the National Front held a demonstration, the communists came along to throw bricks and stones. If they could get past the police, they would attack; and there would be fights. They would say, "You are just the storm troopers of capitalism." That annoyed me. Lots of things annoyed me in those days—but that really annoyed me. It annoyed me because I thought, "Well, I refuse to accept that as a straightforward fight between globalization, multinational corporations, the gospel according to McDonald's, if you like hedonism on one side, and communism on the other." I didn't like either very much, and I refused that the choice had to be that simple.

It was then that someone said to me, "Have you read the distributist ideas of G. K. Chesterton and Hilaire Belloc?" I said, "No, who are they?" And as C. S. Lewis said in *Surprised by Joy,* "A sound atheist cannot be too careful of his reading." The same thing is true of a sound racist—he cannot be too careful of his reading. Actually, I do have one similarity with C. S. Lewis. He was referring to G. K. Chesterton when he wrote that remark in *Surprised by Joy,* with specific reference to *The Everlasting Man.* I was also reading Chesterton. I first read a book called *The Well and the Shallows,* because this person said there is one essay in there you must read. This one essay was two-thirds of the way through the book. Being a methodical sort of person, I started from the beginning anyway. I thought, "If that one essay is worth reading, the rest should be worth reading." In that book, *The Well and the Shallows,* the rest of those essays were a defense of Catholicism from various attacks upon it—mostly modern rationalist, secular attacks upon it. It was written in 1935, so it included the Nazi racist attacks upon it.

At this time I was involved with all these groups I've mentioned, but I felt that I could not argue with any of what

Chesterton said. When I was reading the book, a Jehovah's Witness knocked on my door. I was living in South London at the time, and I just decided that I would pretend to be a Catholic. It was for an intellectual exercise, a bit of fun, or what have you. Of course, I had nothing to go on except this one book. There is no such thing as a three-minute conversation with a Jehovah's Witness. We had about a half-hour discussion, and at the end of it I was convinced that I had won. I am not arrogant enough to think that he was convinced that I had won, but that's another matter. This was the beginning of my journey.

I had read Chesterton before I went to prison the second time. I fell in love with Chesterton. I could not get enough Chesterton. In those days the Chesterton revival had not gone into full bloom, and indeed the C. S. Lewis revival had not gone into full bloom. It is great to see the revival of interest in both men. You could only get Chesterton books by looking around used bookstores or second-hand book shops.

I bought up a collection of used Chesterton books, and from Chesterton I progressed to Belloc, and from Belloc I progressed to C. S. Lewis, Tolkien, and John Henry Newman. What I can explain is that I never really had what could be called a "Road to Damascus" experience. I did not suddenly fall off my horse blinded and see the light. I had a healing experience. These Christian authors working, if you like, as the agents of the grace of God healed my mind and healed my heart. I was a long way lost, so it took me a long way to get to Limerick, but I got there.

I would say, as well, as a postscript, and as a tribute to my father, that he also was received into the church about seven years ago. He was the original source, perhaps, of my bigotry, and his death this week was wholly beyond my wildest imagining, dreams, and hopes—very prayerful, so neat and tidy. It was not messy at all, and there is no doubt in my mind that my father is in heaven.

Of course, people like Chesterton and Lewis dealt in beauty, but they were also dealing in reason. We must not keep the two separate. We see that both Chesterton and Lewis also wrote works of apologetics—*The Well and the Shallows* is a work of apologetics—but Chesterton also wrote novels, poetry, whimsies, essays, and detective stories. Their works had this essential reason and beauty in them. They wrote beautifully. Few people convey their personality as did Chesterton, whose personality leaps from the page and hugs you.

Lewis, of course, is the same. He wrote apologetics such as *Mere Christianity*, but also wonderful works of literature, such as Chronicles of Narnia, The Ransom Trilogy, *Till We Have Faces, The Great Divorce*. These are all wonderful works of beauty that also convey reason and love, this trinity of truth.

Just to finish, one has to ponder how many thousands, perhaps millions, have been brought to Christ through the writings of C. S. Lewis and G. K. Chesterton. One may also mention Tolkien, T. S. Eliot, Gerard Manley Hopkins, and Evelyn Waugh, great writers of the nineteenth and twentieth centuries. Their writings conveyed beauty in their reason and reason in their beauty, and a love that transcended both. You are looking at one product of their work, but I am one of many thousands.

I want to finish with an anecdote. It is not about me at all, but about someone called Tom Monaghan. I am writer in residence and professor of literature at Ave Maria University in Florida. Ave Maria was founded by Tom Monaghan. If you haven't heard of Tom Monaghan, you have heard of the organization that he started about twenty-five or thirty years ago: Domino's Pizza. He and his brother were orphans. They were poor. He opened a pizza shop in Michigan. It was called Domino's Pizza. The first one had a domino with a one and a zero. The next one was going to have a one and a one, and then a two and a one. Obviously, his hope was to get up to as many as twelve shops. Of course, Domino's Pizza took off and became a multinational corporation. He became very rich. He lived the lifestyle of an extremely wealthy owner of a multinational corporation. He owned helicopters, and countless cars. He owned the Detroit Tigers baseball team. While he owned them, they won the World Series.

Tom Monaghan is a cradle Catholic, but he never left the faith, per se. Instead, he had become lukewarm, indifferent, and of course was living a life that was not necessarily very commensurate with the Christian lifestyle. It was the reading of *Mere Christianity* by C. S. Lewis that changed his life. He had, I think he calls it, a "born again" experience. Having read C. S. Lewis' *Mere Christianity,* he decided that he wanted to die poor. Although it would be difficult for someone that rich to die poor unless he became a manic gambler, he is doing his best, giving money to worthy causes. It was because of this decision that he founded Ave Maria University.

So we talk about this network of minds, and this network of grace. We talk about C. S. Lewis and G. K. Chesterton, but I am standing here because of C. S. Lewis and G. K. Chesterton. I am actually now living in America because of C. S. Lewis, because if it had not been for C. S. Lewis, Tom Monaghan would not have read *Mere Christianity.* If he had not read *Mere Christianity,* he would not have founded Ave Maria University, and I would still be living in England as a poor writer.

So we come back to what this is all about, a network of minds and a network of grace, energizing each other.

The Magpie

With pride the Magpie fills its nest
    with marvelous exotica,
the treasures other envious birds
    long to possess.
What priceless artifacts surround it
    as it sits enthroned
within the lofty palace of its own construction,
    meant to shame its neighbors!
All the while the foolish Robins sing and soar,
    merely enjoying being birds,
when they could amass a rare collection
    instead.

Jackson, Tenn.
February 2004

Made New

A Perspective Beyond Time

Nigel Goodwin

TEXT: Philippians 4:8–9

Let us pray. Lord, may the words of my mouth and the meditation of all of our hearts be acceptable in your sight this night and as we continue on in the joy of knowing you. In Jesus' name, Amen.

Today is the eve of the Feast of Transfiguration, a day on which we remember when Christ took in intimacy three of his closest disciples onto the mountain and revealed to them his glory. And if, by the way, you thought that Moses did not get into the promised land, you thought wrongly, for there was Moses in glory.

I want to read the poem by William Wordsworth that was on our bulletins for the final day. We have heard this morning about mountains being climbed in the Lake District, where Wordsworth lived in Grassmere. It was also the home of the mountain painter, Heaton Cooper, a dear friend who painted the most incredible landscapes, from mountaintop to mountain valley. Wordsworth had this to say of King's College Chapel, the building we are in this evening:

> Tax not the royal saint with vain expense,
> With ill matched aims the architect who planned—
> Albeit laboring, for a scanty band
> Of white-robed scholars only—this immense
> And glorious Work of fine intelligence!
> Give all thou canst; high Heaven rejects the lore
> Of nicely calculated less or more;
> So deemed the man who fashioned for the sense
> These lofty pillars, spread that branching roof
> Self-poised, and scooped in ten thousand cells,
> Where light and shade repose, where music dwells
> Lingering—and wandering on as loathe to die;
> Like thoughts whose very sweetness yieldeth proof
> That they were born for immortality.[1]

Dear friends, each one of you is fearfully and wonderfully made and was born for immortality. We learn of that experience of immortality in this text to Paul's beloved church at Philippi. My theme is "Made New: A Perspective Beyond Time." If Paul the apostle had a favorite among his children, it would have been the church at Philippi. Paul had planted the church himself. It was the first church planted in Europe. Probably both Lydia and the Philippian jailer would have been among the congregation there. They were the beloved, his joy and his crown. Throughout the letter, we discover the throb of a loving heart and the tenderness of a strong man. We have had confirmed to us again and again during the last two weeks of conference together the impossibility of human beings being able to "Make All Things New." An original is the work of the Creator, the Great Artist, and we are little creators under the Creator. As

---

[1] William Wordsworth, "Inside of King's College Chapel, Cambridge," (1821; No. 43, Part III of *Ecclesiastical Sonnets*).

C. S. Lewis says, "the church exists for nothing else but to draw men into Christ, to make them little Christs."[2] That is the dance; that is the choreography!

More than thirty years ago now, the poet Steve Turner said that history repeats itself because no one listens to it.[3]

Humanity cannot "pull its socks up"—however many times a parent may say this to their child. Humanity cannot recreate itself or with scientific, technological, or creative imagination hope to "Make All Things New." There is only one way by which human life may be transformed from death to life, from meaninglessness to meaning, from being helplessly lost to being hopefully found, and that is by becoming a new creation in Christ Jesus.

In Romans 12:2, Paul says, "Do not conform any longer to the pattern of this world, but be transformed by the renewing of your mind" (NIV). There is a radical difference between a catalyst and a chameleon.

My old mentor, Professor Hans Rookmaaker, whom I often quote, said, "Christ did not die to make us—the world—Christian. He died to make us human." In making humankind, God intended perfection. When we were fashioned in his image, we were as he intended us to be, fully human. To "Make All Things New," therefore, and to know what is "Good, True, and Beautiful" is to see the world and to see one another from the perspective of our Maker–in a word, to have the mind of Christ and to think "Christianly."

How is this possible? Paul, in his letter to the Philippian church, gives us a route map for the "how." Just one verse from chapter four, verse eight, is all I shall dwell upon:

Whatsoever things are true,
whatsoever things are honest,
whatsoever things are just,
whatsoever things are pure,

---

[2]C. S. Lewis, *Mere Christianity* (New York: HarperSanFrancisco, 2001), 199.
[3]Steve Turner, "History Lesson," in Up to Date (Tring, U.K.: Lion Publishing, 1976), 129.

whatsoever things are lovely,
whatsoever things are of good report,
if there be any virtue, and if there be any praise,
    think on these things.

This message knows no age barriers and no restraint. It is for each of us. It is, I might say, a fresher and more relevant message today than when first delivered nearly twenty centuries ago.

A number of hearers will be in the plastic period of their lives. The world lies before you, waiting for you to make a difference. A mightier world lies within you to mold as you will. You can be and become almost anything. I don't mean this in regard to externals or even intellectual capacity—these are only partially in our control. I mean this in regard to the more important—the truly real things—vis-à-vis the elevation and the purity of heart and mind! The young among us are reminded by the prophet that "the young men see visions." To ennoble life is to turn the visions into realities. So many of today's youth have the noble desire to save their planet world from the disasters impinged by their parents' and grandparents' generations. Generous and noble ideas, therefore, ought to belong to youth.

Let me cast my thoughts to three simple questions: What? Why? How? Paul asks us, as he did the beloved at Philippi, to "think on these things." This advice implies that we both can and ought to exercise a rigid control over the part of our lives that a great many of us never think of controlling at all. Circumstances, the necessities of daily occupation, duty owed to one another, all these make certain streams of thought necessary and, for some of us, very absorbing. For the rest, it may be said, "He that hath no ruling over his own spirit is like a city that is broken down, and without walls" (Prov. 25:28, KJV). Anyone can go in, and anyone can come out. "How shall we sing the Lord's song in a strange land?" (Ps. 137:4, KJV). In Babylon the captives were told to sing. Sing us one of your songs! Sing us one of your songs! "By the rivers of Babylon, there we sat down, yea, we wept" (Ps. 137:1, KJV).

The Jewish remnant struggles to express itself today. There are in our cities, towns, and nations multitudes who have never considered how responsible they are for the flow of the waves of that great river that comes from the depths of their being. They never ask whether the current is bringing down sand or gold. We must exercise control of the run and drift of our thoughts if we are ever to shape our culture and affect our world. We must put a guard at the gate of the city and a watchman on the walls of our thought processes to let no vagrant in who cannot show a passport and a clean bill of health.

What then is the company of fair guests that the apostle encourages and exhorts us to welcome into the hospitable places in our hearts and minds? "Think on these things." What things?

Whatsoever Things Are True

Our minds must be exercised with truth. They need to be breathed up, braced, lifted, and filled by bringing them into contact with truth, most especially with the highest of all truth, the truth that speaks of God and our relationship with him. Our minds need the truth of which this chapel here in Cambridge speaks. This is a high truth. Our minds must be baptized and soaked in the Word. Jesus introduced many of his important sayings with, "Truly I tell you," (Matt 5:18, 26; 6:2, 5, 16; 8:10; 10:15, 23, 42; 11:11; 13:17; 16:28; 17:20; 18:3, 13, 18-19; 19:23, 28; 21:21, 31; 23:36; 24:2, 34, 47; 25:12, 40, 45; 26:13, 21, 34; Mark 3:28; 8:12; 9:1, 41; 10:15, 29; 11:23; 12:43; 13:30; 14:9, 18, 25, 30; Luke 4:24; 9:27; 12:37, 44; 18:17, 29; 21:3, 32; 23:43; John 1:51; 3:3, 5, 11; 5:19, 24-25; 6:26, 32, 47, 53; 8:34, 51, 58; 10:1, 7; 12:24; 13:16, 20-21, 38; 14:12; 16:20, 23; 21:18 NRSV). Thereby, Jesus claimed to speak "the truth." He went further as he said, "I am ...the truth." (John 14:6). Jesus could speak no other than the truth.

My own mentor, Francis Schaeffer, always spoke, when he stood on his feet, of "True Truth." Today we need to do the same, for when you speak from your grid (frame of reference) to someone else's grid and they smile and nod in agreement, you do not know if they are *hearing* what you are saying unless there is a relationship between you, a dialogue. By "true truth," I mean objective truth, not merely the twenty-first–century existential "feel good factor" subjective truth. "Whatever is true, think on these things."

If you're sitting comfortably tonight, I suspect I am not giving you the truth. I am giving you truth in domesticated form, strawberry flavor. I know you all like strawberry; I quite like it myself. It's nothing but the truth, but it's not the whole truth. No one ever admires the whole truth. It's nice, but where would you put it? People who neglect the strawberry flavor do not get asked back. They get put in their place…with nails if necessary!

Whatsoever Things Are Honest

The word *honest* here can be more properly translated to mean "reverent" or "venerable." Let respectful thoughts be familiar to our minds—genuine, ethical, virtuous, veracious. When wild passions or animal desires dare to cross the threshold of our minds, they can be "awed into silence" and stillness by whatever things are august, notable, worthy; think on these things.

Whatsoever Things Are Just

What things are just? Those things are just that are righteous, fair, impartial, and due, in accordance with the facts, accurate and true.

I was in Birmingham, Alabama, several years ago. There was a judge there who loved Jesus. I said, "How do you, in the law, share grace with those around you?" He said, "When I pronounce sentence upon somebody, I weep over them and afterwards I go to visit them in jail."

Grace and truth came in Jesus Christ and are being lived out by this man. Many of today's young people are passionately concerned for justice whenever they see its opposite being practiced, particularly by governments and departments that claim to be on the side of truth. These things Paul urges all believers to both practice and dwell upon.

Whatsoever Things Are Pure

We who are Christian are called to attend angels with awareness, not unawareness. We are called to a shuddering recoil from impurity so that godly thoughts inhabit our minds. This is a high calling, especially in our twenty-first century that is so driven by the senses, the emotions, and the subjective feelings. It is a calling to a lofty region. The one whose legacy we seek to follow and the cloud of witnesses that surround us call each of us to go both deeper and higher, "further up and further in," as C. S. Lewis said. Only with this Christlike perspective, "Christ in you, the hope of glory," (Col. 1:27), will his Spirit be able to make "All Things New." This then is to be and to become, dear friends, fully Christian, fully human.

Whatsoever Things Are Lovely

Paul is not content here to speak merely of things that are plain and austere. He moves into that which is tinged with emotion—whatever things are lovely. Here again is the theme of our current conference, for goodness is beautiful. In effect, goodness is the *only* beautiful. When the Great Artist, the "us-ness" and "our-ness" God the Creator created, he said, "It is good," and with humankind he said, "It is very good." Very beautiful. This morning from Richard Foster we heard of the *kol Yahweh*, the living voice of God. It is the voice of God that declares what is good. When Jesus was asked what is good, he said, "There is none good but one, that is, God" (Mt. 19:17, KJV). So when the Creator God made what is good, he said, "It is God. It is Spirit. It is *Me*. It is good."

Whatsoever Things Are Admirable (of Good Report)

Whatever things are admirable or of good report, everything that is spoken well of and speaks well in the very naming of, let the thoughts of them be in our minds. Good is not beauty purely in a functional sense. Nor is it merely decorative surface beauty. Rather, it is the fusion of aesthetics and function—a truly lovely world that works and is to be appreciated by all its inhabitants. The fullness and perfection of goodness is Beauty.

Paul concludes by saying, "If there be any virtue…," and here he covers the good of the first four—true, venerable, just, pure. He then adds, "…if there be any praise…," which finally in summing up the last two (lovely and good report), he makes his point: "Think on these things."

Think on These Things

The significance in our own time is that Paul accepts the non-Christian notion of the people in whose tongue he spoke. Here for the only time in his letters he uses the great pagan word "virtue," which was a spell amongst the Greeks. Paul says, in essence, "I accept the world's notion of what is virtuous and praiseworthy, and I ask you, my beloved Christians, to take it to your hearts."

Let us leave at least with the assurance that Christianity covers all the ground that the noblest morality has ever attempted to mask out and to own, and much more besides. Paul is saying, "If there be any virtue, as you Greeks are fond of talking about, and if there be any praise, if there is anything, anything in man that commends noble actions, think on these things." The only way we can do this is to turn away from their opposites.

The great danger since Eden, and dominant in our twenty-first century, is that we dwell on the illusory, the mean, and the frivolous. We are prone to dwell on ugliness and impurity. Like flies we are attracted to putrid meat. The lust and the lewd can draw us all.

Fear of this has taken the church and Christians from the table of transforming their culture to creating a vast Christian dining room of subcultural self-indulgence—ugly eating and working practices. Our voices in the marketplace of ideas are few and scattered, and our irrelevance and impotence are well documented. Our calling in Christ, as I see it, is the legacy of Lewis. It is to engage the world of our generation by being a counterculture with a distinctive mark. As the curtain falls on our gathering together, where will we take the "Good, the True, and the Beautiful" that we have embraced together and digested in relationship one with another these past days at the table of fellowship?

Our service here at King's ends, as does our conference, with holy communion—celebration at the table of our Lord—not as an old script, a faded movie, a forgotten dream, but rather a dynamic, relevant, present, continuous reality. It is the combination of the ingredients of that which is "Good, True, and Beautiful" through the death and resurrection of our Lord in his body and blood at the theater of the cross. This holy celebration, commended by our Lord, puts into each of our hands the cup of promise; we may press into it clusters of ripe grapes and make mellow wine, or we can squeeze into it wormwood and gall and hemlock and poison berries, for as we brew, so we drink. We are called for such a time as this, to be and to become a new creation—people who can transform their culture because they have been transformed themselves. The canvas of our world stands open—empty even—and we may cover it with the figures we most admire. We can do, in our day, as Fra Angelico did in his. He painted the walls of every cell in his quiet monastery with Madonnas, angels, and risen Christs.

"As he thinketh in his heart, so is he" (Prov. 23:7, KJV). Look around your world. See his beautiful space at King's. We see solid, seeming realities of institutions, buildings, governments, inventions, machines, palaces, fortresses, and technological advancements—things of which our great-grandparents hardly dared dream. Everything we see is embodied in thought. There was thought behind each that then took shape. Have any of us who have enjoyed this gathering and previous ones, who have visited C. S. Lewis' home, The Kilns in Oxford, thought what might the C. S. Lewis Foundation build for generations yet to be born; for this reason, in another real sense, the Word become flesh. Thus, our thoughts become visible and stand around us. What a company. What has been the drift and trend of our lives comes out – sometimes in flashes, sometimes in dribbles, but always visible in our actions; as thunder follows lightning, so my acts are neither more nor less than the reverberation and the after-clap of my thoughts.

These Things Do

If we are entertaining in our hearts and minds the precepts of this text, then our lives will be fair and beautiful. The apostle goes on to say, "Those things do" (v. 9). You will if you think about them, and you wont if you don't. I have said, and I will repeat, we keep this counsel by truthfully and radically engaging with Jesus Christ. With him all things are possible for the transformation of our culture. When Jesus said, "You shall know the truth, and the truth shall make you free" (Jn. 8:32, NKJV), he did not add, "and it will hurt." It is, however, the way of the cross. Thinking Christianly is not merely meditating upon abstractions. If Christ is in my thoughts, all good things are there. Remember, all of us who are in Christ were, at one time, not in Him. Christ draws each of us as a magnet to Himself, giving to each of us wings of love and contemplation so we may soar above the earth and walk in heavenly places, not as chirping canaries caught in our cages, but as wild birds who can reach the high peaks.

Set your minds on things that are above, where Christ sits at the right hand of God. If we would allow Christ to be central in the very sanctuary of our minds, then we would, indeed, be a company of blessed people. The very atmosphere in which we move would hum and rattle with the presence of the Divine.

Think on these things.
These things do.
And the God of peace shall be with you.

The poet Luci Shaw has said:

Perform impossibilities
or perish. Thrust out now
the unseasonal ripe figs
among your leaves. Expect
the mountain to be moved.
Hate parents, friends and all
materiality. Love every enemy.
Forgive more times than seventy-
seven. Camel-like, squeeze by
into the kingdom through
the needle's eye. All fear quell.
Hack off your hand, or else,
unbloodied, go to hell.

Thus the divine unreason.
Despairing, you may cry,
with earthy logic—How?
And I, your God, reply:
Leap from your weedy shallows.
Dive into the moving water.
Eye-less, learn to see
truly. Find in my folly your
true sanity. Then, Spirit-driven,
run on my narrow way, sure
as a child. Probe, hold
my unhealed hand, and
bloody, enter heaven.[4]

Amen.

---

[4]Luci Shaw, "The Foolishness of God," *Polishing the Petoskey Stone* (Vancouver: Regent College Publishing, 2003), 198. Used by permission.

The Dogwood Tree

Low branching limbs
designed for childhood's
    little hands
    short arms
    stubby legs
drooping wide like
    a bedouin's tent
    a sailing ship
    a castle
    a fort.

How splendid a palace!
    the playhouse
    for the children of
    a king.

Jackson, Tenn.
May 13, 2004

So What Now?

Rebecca Whitten Poe

TEXT: 2 Timothy 4:1–5

So what now? We have spent this time filling our minds with "everything true, everything noble, everything right, everything pure, everything lovely, everything admirable...excellent or praiseworthy." We have thought about "such things." So what do we do now that our minds are full?

Paul and Timothy do not let us wonder long; in the following verse of their letter to the Philippians, they write that we are simply to take all we have learned and "put it into practice" (Phil. 4:9, NIV). As Jesus said, "out of the overflow of [the] heart [the] mouth speaks" (Lk. 6:45, NIV). Our hearts are full—we need to let them overflow! We are to be true, noble, and pure, representing Christ in our actions and our words. If we "think on such things," then we have a responsibility to reflect them in our lives.

This responsibility has never been more challenging. In the postmodern world in which we live, the definition of the good, the true, and the beautiful has been blurred and warped almost past recognition. Those who profess to believe in absolutes are condemned as judgmental, while those with no standards are called tolerant. To be open-minded is to be intellectual and mature, and among young people, it is the highest achievable praise. How can we argue with such close-minded open-mindedness?

I recently had the opportunity to study, briefly, in Italy. I am fairly well traveled for a person of my age, and I have already noticed the common discrepancy between the idyllic pictures of various places and the reality. Italy defied my skepticism: it *looked* like Italy. The countryside varied from region to region but was consistently gorgeous. Each city had different characteristics but each city was stunning in its own way. I was in a constant state of awe as I saw the beautiful buildings and pieces of art that are enduring reminders that the "grandeur that was Rome" has yet to die. The fact that so many of the great structures still have such an imposing presence astounds me. If the mere ruins of ancient Rome render modern visitors (jaded by skyscrapers and suspension bridges) speechless, what must first- or second-century travelers to that city have felt?

Just past the Roman Forum stands a small prison that is hardly more than a hole in the rock. In the first century A.D., the only entrance to the underground prison chamber was a small opening, only about a foot across, in the guard chamber floor; the only way out was almost invariably an execution order. It was in this cold, dark prison that the apostle Paul spent his last days. He did not have his friend Timothy with him this time; he was alone. Many of his other friends had deserted him, and he knew he was about to die. Rather than bemoan his lot, however, as many of us would be wont to do, he penned his final letter to Timothy, encouraging him and challenging him in his ministry:

> In the presence of God and of Christ Jesus, who will judge the living and the dead, and in view of his appearing and his kingdom, I give you this charge: Preach the Word; be prepared in season and out of season; correct, rebuke and encourage—with great patience and careful instruction. For the time will come when men will not put up with sound doctrine. Instead, to suit their own desires, they

will gather around them a great number of teachers to say what their itching ears want to hear. They will turn their ears away from the truth and turn aside to myths. But you, keep your head in all situations, endure hardship, do the work of an evangelist, discharge all the duties of your ministry. (2 Tim. 2:1—5, NIV)

Until I went to Rome, I did not fully understand the polytheistic threat that challenged the growth of Christianity in the first centuries after Christ. I was struck by how much of the artwork and architecture that survives from ancient times has a religious significance. The Capitoline Hill alone was literally covered with temples, large and small. It is easy to see what a culture values: you just have to observe where their money is spent. Humans have a great need and appreciation for religion. We crave what is good and true and beautiful, whether we choose to acknowledge this fact or not. The problem is not the craving, but rather the ways in which we chose to satisfy our "itching ears."

Like the people about whom Paul warned Timothy, we today have a dangerous tendency to "turn aside to myths." Often I think we are seduced by the beauty of them. The temples and statues I saw in Rome were much more appealing than the bare prison cell from which Paul sent out his challenge. No one in their right mind would willingly choose to serve their God in Marmion Prison rather than the Parthenon. In the twenty-first century, it is so easy to forget what God considers good and true and beautiful when all around us the world displays its corruption of them. When I constantly see tall and tanned women portrayed as the ideal of feminine beauty, for example, it is easy for me (a fair-skinned young woman under five feet tall) not to recognize beauty in myself. When little boys repeatedly see killers or thieves characterized as "the good guys" in movies, it is easy for them not to respect the authority of the police. When youth grow up in an age of sarcasm and cynicism, it is easy for them not to appreciate truth when they hear it.

My biblical Greek professor, Dr. Ray Van Neste, once made an astute observation about the English language, which I think applies to our culture as well. We were discussing the fact that different Greek words that have the same meaning may be used interchangeably in a text without any real exegetical significance. Dr. Van Neste remarked that some words might have a more forceful connotation in the Greek, however, which can be lost when translated into English. He explained:

> The English language has been in many ways "dumbed-down." We use such emphatic words so easily that they soon lose their power. For example, if after asking a professor how you did on his test he replies to you "good," then most conscientious students would begin to worry. "Good" no longer articulates high quality. "Good" now means "passable," while one must progress to "great" in order to put nervous students' minds at rest.

In this postmodern world, so many of our values have been "dumbed down" and rendered ambiguous because of overuse and misuse. Good has been diluted, truth has been distorted, and beauty has been cheapened. Twenty-first–century "mythology" seduces us. The outpouring of values through the media has an important role to play in understanding my generation's perception of what is good, true, and beautiful.

As a college student, I have a "front-row seat" to my generation's reevaluation of the good, the true, and the beautiful. (And we *are* reevaluating these ideas—we are rebellious!) For better or for worse, I have grown up in an age of mass media and the exponential evolution of technology. Conversation and recreation alike would most likely grind to a halt on my college campus without movies and sitcoms to discuss or I-pods and MP3 players on which to play music. And I attend a college where almost every student is a Christian!

These forms of entertainment have become such integral parts of everyday life for us. The proof? When four well-educated, well-rounded college students spend an entire semester attempting to figure out what placement of furniture in a living room provides the best view of the television set, I think it is safe to say that the media has become an integral part of everyday life. Even more proof: we moved the dinner table *out* of the apartment because there was just not room for it *and* the television. Dinner has been an integral part of human social experience since the dawn of human relationships, yet now media takes precedence over what is one of the most enjoyable aspects of life.

Well, "there is nothing new under the sun." Is our current obsession with media so different from the ancients' obsession with religion? In those times, it was common for a person to choose their favorite deity to worship, and there were many cults from which to choose! Remember what Paul said when he was in Athens, which was by then a part of the Roman Empire?

> "Men of Athens! I see that in every way you are very religious. For as I walked around and looked carefully at your objects of worship, I even found an altar with this inscription: TO AN UNKNOWN GOD" (Acts 17:22—23, NIV).

My generation is very religious, as well. Our altars, however, are not made of stone but of televisions; our gods and goddesses are not marble but pop stars. What we see in the media so pervades our society and minds that we often have a difficult time differentiating media from reality. We are, however, a generation of seekers, not simply mindless viewers. We look for purpose and meaning in everything, and the "cults" that spring up from the media represent our beliefs and values.

Take *Star Wars,* for example. For almost three decades, it has been a fundamental piece of American pop culture. Even my friends who have never seen these movies are familiar with the storyline and easily recognize and understand allusions to it. *Star Wars* could perhaps be called the defining movie of the twentieth century. For those who are not familiar with the story, I will point out an instance of what I mean. Obi-Wan Kenobi, the mentor of the hero Luke Skywalker, explained to the young

Luke early in the story that the evil Darth Vader had killed Luke's father. Luke later discovers that Darth Vader *is* his father and challenges Obi-Wan's lie. Obi-Wan calmly defends his rationale by asserting that what he said was "true, from a certain point of view." When Luke's father was seduced and corrupted by the dark side of the Force to become Darth Vader, the good man that he was died.

It sounds tempting, does it not: "true, from a certain point of view?" There is no absolute truth here; it all depends upon your viewpoint. No pressure, no guilt. How can we tell people to think on what is true if their interpretation of truth is the opposite of ours? Paul's warning to Timothy comes down to us across the centuries: "To suit their own desires [men have gathered] around them a great number of teachers to say what their itching ears want to hear. They [have turned] their ears away from the truth and turned aside to myths This is the challenge that faces us.

There is, however, hope. *The Lord of the Rings* and the *Harry Potter* books have achieved cult status almost equal to that of *Star Wars,* yet they portray good and evil as two separate and opposing forces. The use of the Ring, for example, will always result in destruction: "[They] cannot use it, and what is done with it turns to evil."[1] Fortunately, Peter Jackson did not choose to omit this idea when adapting Tolkien's books for film. My generation has much to learn even from the much-debated *Harry Potter* books:

> Harry gets in trouble like any normal child, but he realizes when he has done something wrong. Much more, he regrets doing things wrong. Most remarkable of all, Harry Potter believes that such a thing as wrong exists. He is truly a magical child!…Harry Potter has no room for relativistic mish mosh. His villains are evil. Evil is not good. It is bad. Harry can make value judgments

[1] J. R. R. Tolkien, *The Fellowship of the Ring* (New York: Ballantine Books, 1973), 468.

because right and wrong, good and evil, true and false actually exist. He may not always know what to do about the evil in his world, but he suffers from no delusion that evil is relative. Because Harry can recognize evil and falsehood in the most wicked and diabolical villain in his world, he can also recognize it in its simplest form in the people around him like the other students in his school. He can even recognize it in himself…Lord Voldemort may believe that there is no right and wrong, only power, but Harry Potter knows he is wrong. If children believe Harry, then the crack in the dyke has been plugged.[2]

Such obvious moral absolutism in the modern media is an encouragement to me. Thanks to the popularity of *Lord of the Rings, Harry Potter,* and even the newly released Chronicles of Narnia, there is now a precedent in our society for absolute truth, goodness, and beauty. The dyke is steadily being plugged.

And this pervasive moral relativism in our society is not the only "myth." Nor, according to C. S. Lewis, is it the original "myth." In a letter he wrote to Arthur Greeves he described a moment of enlightenment:

Now what Dyson and Tolkien showed me was this: that if I met the idea of sacrifice in a Pagan story I didn't mind it at all: again, that if I met the idea of a god sacrificing himself to himself…I liked it very much and was mysteriously moved by it: again, that the idea of the dying god and reviving god…similarly moved me provided I met it anywhere *except* in the Gospels… Now the story of Christ is simply a true myth: a myth working on us in the same way as the others, but with the tremendous difference that *it really happened*…Pagan stories are God expressing Himself through the minds of poets, using such images as He found there, while

[2]Harry Lee Poe, "Harry's 'wizardry': bedrock values," *Commercial Appeal,* Sunday, November 27, 2005, V-3.

Christianity is God expressing Himself through what we call "real things."[3]

In *Surprised by Joy,* Lewis clarifies his view of the relationship between the "true myth" and the "pagan stories":

> The comparison is of course between something of infinite moment and something very small; like comparison between the Sun and the Sun's reflection in a dewdrop. Indeed, in my view, very like it, for I do not think the resemblance between the Christian and the merely imaginative experience is accidental. I think that all things, in their way, reflect heavenly truth, the imagination not least.[4]

Humans do have "itching ears," and we try desperately to find a way to scratch them. We try to catch glimmering reflections of what is good, true, and beautiful, but, like any reflection in water, the image is distorted. Even the pagan Plato recognized this truth when writing his "Allegory of the Cave." So many of my generation are chained in a cave watching shadows on the wall, believing that what they see is reality. We who have broken out of the cave must "do the work of [evangelists], [discharging] all the duties of [our] ministry." But how to convince a generation that has never seen the true light that there is more to life than the shadows they now worship?

The answer is just what Paul and Timothy write to the Philippians. We must "put into practice" the beliefs and values we cherish. It will be a slow process; we must "endure hardship," remember? It may be that only one person will slowly rise into the light at a time. It is not enough, however, for us to sit and simply *consider* the implications of "Making All Things New: The Good, the True, and the Beautiful in the Twenty-first Century" when Christ commanded us to "go into all the world" with him as he makes "all things new."

---

[3]Walter Hooper, ed., *The Collected Letters of C. S. Lewis,* vol. 1 (San Francisco: Harper Collins, 2004), 974–76.

[4]C. S. Lewis, *Surprised by Joy* (New York: Harcourt, Inc., 1955), 167.

Cambridge Afternoon

I search the crowd in vain to find a welcome and
    familiar face;
Now that those, once friendship formed, have
    scattered from this antique place
of stone and brick, and slate and lead, of cap and
    gown, and learned grace.
Beside the chapel, down the road, across the street,
    within the church;
I catch a glimpse of someone who for fourteen days
    was dear to me;
And then with melancholy eye I see it was not he
    nor was it she.

Great St. Mary's Church
Cambridge
August 1, 1998